THE SMARTER ACCOUNTANT

How To Eliminate Stress and Overwhelm, Create More Time, Gain a Competitive Advantage, and More!

DAWN GOLDBERG, CPA

DEDICATION AND THANK YOU

This book is dedicated to all the current and future accountants who want a successful career without having to sacrifice a life. It's for every accountant who wasn't taught how their brain works and how they have been underutilizing it. It's for every accountant on the verge of burnout who wants to know a better way.

A huge thank you to my husband, John Sinnott, for always supporting and believing in me. Thank you for being "my person" and taking this wild ride with me.

Much gratitude to my parents for always loving and supporting me, no matter what. I wouldn't be where I am without having the foundation you provided.

Finally, a huge thank you to Brooke Castillo, the founder of The Life Coach School. You changed my life in more ways than you cannot imagine, and now I get to change the accounting profession because of you.

CONTENTS

PART I - THE PROCESS   6

Chapter One: Introduction   7
- The Boxes Most Accountants Check   7
- My Story   9
- Why I Wrote This Book   9
- Why You Should Read This Book   12
- How This Book Is Organized   13
- How To Use This Book   14
- My Hope For You   15

Chapter Two: The Formula   17
- How I Discovered The Formula   17
- Accountants Are On The Verge Of Major Burnout   19
- Understanding Your Accountant's Brain   22
- Using The Higher Part Of Your Brain More Intentionally   25
- Before We Move On   27

Chapter Three: The Model   28
- Barbara's Story   28
- The Power Of The Model For Accountants   29
- What Is The Model?   31
- Before We Move On   40

PART II—UNCHECKING THE BOXES   42

Chapter One: Introduction   43

Chapter Two: If I'm So Smart, Why Do I Feel So Stressed and Overwhelmed, Especially During Deadlines?   46
- Mary's Story   46
- The Truth About Stress and Overwhelm   47
- Unchecking the Box   48
- Summary   51

Chapter Three: If I'm So Smart, Why Do I Work Too Many Hours?   54
- Joe's Story   54
- The Truth About Working Too Many Hours   55
- Unchecking the Box   57

Summary	61
Chapter Four: If I'm So Smart, Why Is My Life So Unbalanced and My Time Management Such an Issue?	**63**
Lisa's Story	63
The Truth About Balance and Time Management	64
Unchecking the Box	67
Summary	70
Chapter Five: If I'm So Smart, Why Am I Not as Productive as I'd Like to Be?	**73**
Jeff's Story	73
The Truth About Productivity	74
Unchecking the Box	76
Summary	79
Chapter Six: If I'm So Smart, Why Do I Get Stuck Comparing Myself to Others?	**82**
Kendra's Story	82
The Truth About Comparing and Despairing	83
Unchecking the Box	86
Summary	90
Chapter Seven: If I'm So Smart, Why Do I Have Such Difficulty With Criticism?	**92**
Mark's Story	92
The Truth About Criticism	93
Unchecking the Box	95
Summary	99
Chapter Eight: If I'm So Smart, Why Am I Not Making The Money I Want?	**102**
Danielle's Story	102
The Truth About Money	103
Unchecking the Box	106
Summary	110
Chapter Nine: If I'm So Smart, Why Are My Relationships So Difficult?	**113**
Rob's Story	113
The Truth About Relationships	114
Unchecking the Box	118
Summary	121
Chapter Ten: If I'm So Smart, Why Is Work Affecting My Health?	**124**
Heather's Story	124
The Truth About Your Health	125
Unchecking the Box	128
Summary	132

Chapter Eleven: If I'm So Smart, Why Do I Struggle With Self-Confidence, Self-Doubt, and Imposter Syndrome?	135
Adam's Story	135
The Truth About Self-Confidence, Self-Doubt, and Imposter Syndrome	136
Unchecking the Box	139
Summary	143
Chapter Twelve: If I'm So Smart, Why Do I Have Difficulty Setting Boundaries and Detaching From Work?	145
Gina's Story	145
The Truth About Setting Boundaries and Detaching From Work	146
Unchecking the Box	149
Summary	152
Chapter Thirteen: If I'm So Smart, Why Don't I Feel Happier/Better?	155
Brian's Story	155
The Truth About Feeling Happier/Better	156
Unchecking the Box	158
Summary	162
Chapter Fourteen: If I'm So Smart, Why (Fill In The Blank)?	164
Your Story	164
PART III - THE PLAN	**166**
Chapter One: The Final Story	167
Jim's Story	167
Chapter Two: The Life Of A Smarter Accountant	169
Chapter Three: Gaining A Competitive Advantage	172
Chapter Four: Why This Matters	174
Chapter Five: The Two Options	176

PART I - THE PROCESS

CHAPTER ONE: INTRODUCTION

The Boxes Most Accountants Check

This book is about what you never learned in school, in any CPA exam prep course, in any accounting CPE seminar, or in any business building workshop.

This book is about your accountant brain - the most important asset you have and how you're underutilizing it.

Let's face it, you're already smart, or you wouldn't be an accountant. You probably have a pretty high IQ, and when you're not in a CPE seminar with other accountants, you're probably one of the smartest people in the room.

But here's the hard truth - you aren't using your brain to the best of its ability.

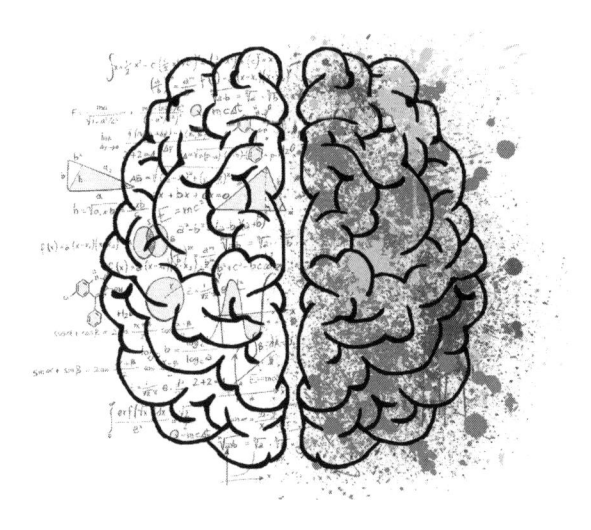

How would you know? Check to see if any of these apply:

- ☐ You feel stressed and overwhelmed, especially during deadlines.
- ☐ You work too many hours.
- ☐ Your life is unbalanced, and you wish you had better time management.
- ☐ You're not as productive as you'd like to be.
- ☐ You compare yourself to others.
- ☐ You have difficulty with criticism.
- ☐ You're not making the money you want to make.
- ☐ You have difficulty with some of your relationships.
- ☐ Your work is affecting your health.
- ☐ You struggle with self-confidence, self-doubt, and imposter syndrome.
- ☐ You have difficulty setting boundaries and detaching from work.
- ☐ You wish you could feel happier/better.

Whether you've been an accountant for many years, or just starting out, I promise you that you're underutilizing your brain if you checked any of the above boxes.

How do I know? Because once I discovered what I'm going to share with you, everything changed for me, both professionally and personally.

Why should you become a Smarter Accountant? Because everything you want is on the other side. You need to learn how you are underutilizing your accountant's brain and what to do about it.

My Story

For most of my public accounting career, I checked all those boxes at various times. But a few years ago, I discovered the formula that changed everything.

I was able to eliminate stress (yes, even during tax season!), I was able to reduce overwhelm (yes, even with all the changes that COVID-19 brought to our personal lives and our work as accountants), and one by one, I began unchecking those boxes that seem to typically affect accountants.

The funny thing is that I had initially been applying the formula to other areas of my life, believing, like most of you, that stress and overwhelm were just par for the course for accountants. I believed that it was part of what accountants needed to deal with; in a strange way, it was necessary to get our work done.

But once I saw how the formula had improved every other area of my life, I decided to apply it to the most stressful thing in a public accountant's career - tax season. I figured, if the formula worked, then why not test it on the biggest hurdle there was. And it worked!

Why I Wrote This Book

I was recently interviewed for a podcast and was asked when I knew I wanted to be an accountant. I immediately remembered the bookkeeping class I took in 10th grade in 1982. I did very well and was encouraged to study accounting in college.

Unlike some of my high school bookkeeping classmates, I just loved how there was always an answer in accounting. I loved the problem-solving aspect of accounting, where you just needed to figure out the best way to get the answer.

Once I graduated Magna Cum Laude from the private college I attended, I was offered positions with 6 out of the Big 8 firms (yes, there were 8 back then). I chose to work at Deloitte (Deloitte Haskins & Sells at the time) in the Tax Department because during the office tour, a classmate from my college, who was a year ahead of me, pulled me aside and said, "Go into Tax. Don't choose Audit!"

During my 30+ year career in public accounting, I worked 10 years for Deloitte in the Tax Department, worked a year or so for Ernst & Young in the Tax Department, took 2 years off after my second child was born, and have worked in a small firm for over 20 years.

So, if you do the math, that means I've had decades of tax seasons under my belt. But honestly, I spent most of them as miserable and stressed as you can imagine.

Like you, I gradually began checking all those boxes on the previous page throughout my accounting career. Everyone in my family knew to "leave Dawn alone" at those stressful times of the year. All of my coworkers, bosses, and fellow CPE attendees agreed that tax season is stressful, accounting is a challenging career, and (fill in your own blank with what makes accounting difficult).

Like most accountants, I blamed things like the profession, the IRS, the clients, and even the dates on the calendar, for things like how I was feeling (unhappy), what I could and couldn't do (accountants don't get to go skiing), and the results I seemed to be stuck with (not enough time with my kids).

Thankfully, all that changed when I discovered and implemented the formula I will share with you. The best part is that I'm not a special unicorn; I can and will teach it to you so you can start unchecking those boxes as I did.

Once I learned and applied the formula, I knew I needed to share it with other accountants, especially accountant moms. Therefore, the next step in my journey was to take my earlier life coaching certification (something I decided to study for 3 years in my "free time", while also working as a CPA and raising my two children) and figure out how to help as many accountant moms as I could.

The best way I knew how was to start a coaching business, The CPA Moms' Coach, and start The CPA Moms' Podcast. I didn't want to keep this important information to myself, so I started marketing and trying to reach as many accountant moms as possible.

The funny thing is that I had no idea that the company, CPA MOMS®, already existed to help match talented accountant moms with entrepreneurs that needed their services. Once the founder and CEO of CPA MOMS, Mayumi Young, CPA, reached out to me, we discovered our shared vision, and I became their Community Manager (in addition to my continued Accounting career).

I am proud to say that, as of the writing of this book, The CPA MOMS Podcast has over 200 episodes and counting, with over 100,000 downloads. My message and motivation have always been clear - accountants need to know the formula for how to be a Smarter Accountant and how to stop underutilizing their accountant's brains.

Although I had been marketing solely to accountant moms, coaching a few accountant dads along the way, it became clear that ALL accountants needed to know how to be a Smarter Accountants, not just accountant moms. I could see that the accounting profession at large was on the verge of a nervous breakdown, especially post-pandemic, and I knew I could definitely help.

To borrow a sentiment from Oprah, here's what I know for sure - the world needs Smarter Accountants; not burned out, stressed out, frustrated accountants that dread going to work, who are overwhelmed by everything happening both professionally and personally, and who are considering walking away from the profession. Your company, clients, and family need you to learn the skill I'm about to teach you.

Now more than ever, we all need to have a clear-cut way to not succumb to burnout, to be able to handle the never-ending changes that come with our profession and to be the best accountants we can be. Accountants need support, and I know what will make all the difference - learning how to be a Smarter Accountant.

Why You Should Read This Book

Once you understand the step-by-step formula that I'll be teaching you in this book and you've practiced and applied it, you can expect to uncheck those previous boxes and start checking these instead:

- Feel less stressed and overwhelmed, especially during deadlines.
- Not work so many hours because you'll get more done in less time.
- Have a more balanced life (whatever balance means to you).

- Be more productive and efficient,
- Stop comparing yourself to others.
- Be able to handle criticism.
- Make more money.
- Improve your relationships.
- Improve your health by reducing stress and overwhelm.
- Feel more confident.
- Be able to set better boundaries and detach from work when you're not at work.
- Feel happier/better.

If you want a competitive advantage, this book will show you how (more on that later). To stand out from the crowd, you need to begin addressing the things that have been getting in the way. This book will show you the way.

How This Book Is Organized

Part I will teach you the step-by-step formula and show you the power of being a Smarter Accountant. I will walk you through how I, and my coaching clients, have used the formula to become Smarter Accountants.

Part II will teach how to specifically apply the formula to each box you initially checked in the Introduction. The best part is, if you checked a box (or boxes), you'll be able to learn the formula in Part I and then go to the section in Part II that specifically shows you how to apply it to that issue.

How To Use This Book

Before we dive in, you first need to know that the only way to become a Smarter Accountant is to do the work. If there's one thing I see repeatedly, it's accountants arguing for their limitations.

This means you believe that things like stress and overwhelm are just par for the course for accountants, and you tend to argue that that's just the way it is for accountants. I'm here to tell you that that is a lie.

When you become a Smarter Accountant, you'll see through the lies you've been telling yourself about what is "normal" for accountants. You'll be able to have the career and the life you want.

Once you learn what I'm going to teach you, you'll gradually be able to see how much control you have over things in your work and personal life and how to achieve any goals you've set.

Time and time again, my coaching clients tell me, "You do know that this is life-changing, right?". To which I answer time and time again, "I know! That's why more accountants need to know this".

Once you understand the formula, you'll be able to apply it to any of those checked boxes and honestly, to any situation you're faced with in your professional and personal life.

If you're the kind of person who likes to learn by example and want to see the formula for being a Smarter Accountant in action first, feel free to read Part II, then come back through Part I to understand how to become a Smarter Accountant.

I promise you that by the time you finish this book, learning the formula in Part I and then seeing it applied in Part II, you will discover what's been getting in your way. You'll be able to have the accounting career, and the life for that matter, that you truly want and deserve.

My Hope For You

As I said before, this formula has changed every area of my life, and I know it can change yours too. I hope that in learning how to be a Smarter Accountant, you will not just tolerate your career, but thrive in your career. I hope that you become the person others say, "Wow, you've changed (for the better). What's the secret?".

I hope that by reading this book, you'll see how you are underutilizing your brain, how there's so much more you are in control of than you realize, and that understanding how to be a Smarter Accountant will change how you work and live.

I also hope you become an example of what's possible for other accountants who have the same struggles you had; that learning how to be a Smarter Accountant, it opens the door to more options than you previously had. No matter where you are in your accounting career when you learn to become a Smarter Accountant, you also expand your options as well.

The best part about this book is that once you understand and apply the formula, you'll see it affecting every other area of your life, not just your accounting career. Once you understand how to be a

Smarter Accountant, you'll also be a smarter woman, man, mother, father, friend, sister, brother, etc.

I promise you that once you understand how you have been underutilizing your accountant's brain, and how to start utilizing it in a smarter way, everything will change for the better. You'll be so happy that you chose to read this book and apply what you'll learn.

CHAPTER TWO: THE FORMULA

How I Discovered The Formula

A number of years ago, I came across a book titled *If I'm So Smart, Why Can't I Lose Weight*, by Brooke Castillo. The title was intriguing, and like most women, I was open to discovering a better way to lose weight. In this book, she talked about something she called the "Self-Coaching Model". I was intrigued but didn't do much with her suggestions.

Then years later, I came across another book she wrote titled *Self-Coaching 101,* and it talked more in-depth about the Self-Coaching Model from the earlier book and how to apply it. Now I was intrigued even more, so I decided to understand it better and apply it.

As all busy accountants and parents can attest to, life got hectic, and I put the book on the shelf, promising myself that once I had more time, I would work on it. A few years went by, and those two books sat on my shelf, along with many other promising books, just waiting for my life to get less hectic (as if).

Fast forward a few years more, and I discover that Brooke not only has a podcast called "The Life Coach School Podcast," but also started a life coaching school (this was after I had already become certified as a life coach from a different school). For some reason, I was finally ready to hear what she had been trying to teach me with each book that sat on my shelf.

I listened to each podcast episode, absorbing what she taught about how to better utilize our brains. When she offered listeners the opportunity to join her new program called "Self-Coaching Scholars," I knew it was what I needed to do. I knew I would never "find" the time, that I needed to make the time.

In the monthly program, we were given a workbook on a different topic each month, had daily homework that tied to that month's topic, had the opportunity to watch or participate in weekly coaching calls via Zoom, and could use a message board to ask any questions we had about the material. This was when everything changed for me.

As I diligently did my daily homework (as all good accountants would do), attended weekly coaching sessions where I was coached, and watched others being coached, I realized how many things were improving in my life. I was doing the suggested 15 - 20 minutes of homework a day and seeing significant changes.

The funny thing was, that other people were noticing the changes as well. I was less stressed, I wasn't bothered by so many people, places, and things, I was more focused at work, I got more done in less time, and I was less reactionary, to name just a few of the many changes.

Based on everything I witnessed in my own life, I eventually decided to reignite my passion for helping others and helping accountant moms struggling to balance their careers with their families. I chose to study for an additional coach certification with Brooke at The Life Coach School and have permission to use her Model as the formula for helping my coaching clients manage their accountant's brains.

After working together for just a few weeks, clients saw changes both professionally and personally. They were improving their relationships, drastically reducing their level of stress, managing their schedule better, leaving jobs that no longer suited them, finding jobs that they had never permitted themselves to dream about, transitioning from being an employee to an entrepreneur, and being better able to handle any changes that life threw at them.

As I said before, one day, I realized that what I had been teaching needed to be shared with ALL accountants, not just the amazing accountant moms that had been listening to The CPA MOMS Podcast or the ones I had the pleasure of coaching. I knew that *EVERY* accountant could benefit from learning the formula for managing their minds.

So, whether you're an accounting student, a college graduate, male, female, employee, or entrepreneur - if you are going to be, or already are, an accountant, learning the formula for how to be a Smarter Accountant will be be a game-changer. It might sound melodramatic, but I think it's the secret to everything!

Whether you're a fan of The CPA MOMS podcast or not, here's what I tell my audience and my clients - when you learn how to manage your mind, you can manage everything else.

Accountants Are On The Verge Of Major Burnout

This book is so important is that, even before COVID-19, accountants struggled with burnout. Mental health has become such a significant health crisis that every year, during the first week of October, the organization NAMI (National Alliance on Mental Health) participates in raising awareness of mental health issues nationwide.

They work to educate the public, fight mental-health stigmas, and support those with mental health issues. Their message is vital, especially in this post-pandemic world that we're all struggling to make sense of.

While the conversation about mental health is becoming less and less taboo, it's still an issue for many, especially in the accounting profession. The subject of workplace well-being is being addressed more because it's becoming an even bigger issue in the accounting and finance professions.

In one study by the Chartered Accountants Benevolent Association, 30.4% of accountants admitted to suffering from mental health issues, and 51% admitted that depression and anxiety leave them dreading going to work. The study shared that workplace stress had caused 42% of respondents to consider resigning, 40% had looked for a new job elsewhere, and nearly one in seven (14%) had handed in their notice because of workplace stress.

Depending on how long you've been working in the accounting profession, you may have also experienced the normalization of anxiety from most of the people you work with. Attending an in-person continuing education seminar with other overwhelmed, anxious accountants can seem like a "we're all in this together" club.

The good news is that anxiety is a natural response that your primitive brain has when it senses fear and uses this response for your survival (you'll learn more about your primitive brain in a bit).

When you feel anxious, there is nothing wrong with you because your brain is only trying to protect you from perceived danger.

The bad news is that your brain interprets danger in many more non-dangerous situations than you realize. A tax deadline, an unexpected science project for your middle-schooler, or a delayed train can create the same feeling of danger that a saber-toothed tiger did when humans lived in caves.

The real problem for accountants is that from the time we went to school to study accounting, we have been trained to think in specific ways, which can often create unnecessary stress and anxiety. Your accountant's brain has been trained for the problem-solving work you do, and when it goes unchecked, it can become your default way of thinking about everything.

If you've ever been told that you are thinking, talking, or arguing like an accountant, that's what I'm talking about. You have been trained to think in ways non-accountants don't think and don't understand.

Being surrounded by other people's problems trains your accountant's brain to see more problems. Since your brain is already a problem-solving machine, when you add that capability to the accounting profession's pressures and expectations, it's no wonder over 50% of accountants feel anxiety and overwhelmed.

One of the methods many accountants use to self-medicate when it comes to anxiety is ironically overworking. This creates an unhealthy relationship with work where you believe that being anxious is fueling you to get more work done or that it shows that you care about what you are doing.

Like the relationship between an addict and a drug dealer, accounting environments notoriously supply and encourage overworking, especially in public accounting. The external pressures to do more, learn more, and be more can slowly begin to ignite burnout.

I believe this issue has only been exacerbated since the pandemic shifted so much of what we had normalized. The incredible stress and pressure that most accountants recently experienced since the 2020 financial crisis has brought the importance of mental health even more to the forefront of important issues for accountants to address.

I hope that you, the reader, will share this book with other accountants and that we cannot feel so ashamed and alone in our collective stress and overwhelm. I want all accountants to understand how to utilize their brains to insulate them from the typical challenges that financial professionals cope with.

I want every accounting student and practicing accountant to start unchecking those boxes you checked in the Introduction to this book. I want you to be a Smarter Accountant so that this and every generation of accountants can handle the changes and challenges that will come our way differently than they've been handled in the past.

Understanding Your Accountant's Brain

One of the most important things I've learned in my studies with The Life Coach School is how our brains work. Like I said before, none of what I'm going to share with you was taught in any accounting class, seminar, or training I've ever attended.

Before understanding what I'm going to share, I had no idea how much control I had over so many things in my professional and personal life. Just like you, I had normalized many of those boxes you checked in the Introduction.

So, to provide an overview of what I learned, it's important to understand something about your human brain - we have two main operating systems going on in our brains that we need to get familiar with. Knowing the difference between the two and understanding how to manage them is going to be the starting point to help you become a Smarter Accountant.

In Nobelist Daniel Kahneman's bestseller, *Thinking, Fast and Slow*, he describes the two systems in our brain as simply System 1 and System 2. I was taught that System 1 is your primitive brain and System 2 is your higher brain.

In the simplest terms possible, System 1, your primitive brain, runs the show more than 80% of the time. This part of your brain is referred to as the reptilian brain and has anatomically been with us since before we were cave dwellers.

One of the key elements to understand is that this primitive part of your brain is motivated by three things (also referred to as the Motivational Triad):

1. Seek pleasure;
2. Avoid pain;

3. Be efficient/save energy;

System 1's job is to keep you safe and alive, and it takes that job very seriously. It releases feel-good chemicals when it interprets that pleasure is present, it releases fear-based chemicals when it senses danger is present, and it likes things to be in familiar, comfortable patterns.

It's the part of the brain that I often refer to as the "Toddler" because it throws a temper tantrum whenever something doesn't fall into one of those 3 categories - it needs to be pleasurable, not painful, and familiar, or else. This toddler part of the brain is all about immediate gratification and doesn't think in terms of the "big picture" or in the long-term.

System 1 sees many of the challenges that accountants face as life-threatening and will typically throw up huge warning flares. Since its job is to keep you safe, and most of the challenges accountants deal with do *NOT* fall into the category of pleasure (i.e., deadlines) or efficiency (i.e., needing to learn new things constantly), then they must be avoided, according to System 1.

On the other hand, System 2 is the prefrontal cortex, a higher-level part of the brain that is only present in humans. The superpower of this part of your human brain is that it allows you to think about what you think about, and it can manage the primitive brain of System 1.

I like to refer to System 2 as the "Supervising Mother/Father" because this part of your brain can think rationally and can see the big picture benefits that the Toddler can't. System 2 is the part of the brain you use to make decisions and is one of the most underutilized parts of your accountant's brain because you're often reacting with the primitive brain, or System 1.

The good news is that you can use System 2 to override System 1, allowing you to face and conquer any challenges that arise and helping you deal with the negative effects of the Motivational Triad. This is why brain management and the formula I'm going to teach you are so incredibly important, especially for accountants.

Brain management is understanding how these two systems can be managed and mastered to uncheck those boxes and become a Smarter Accountant. It's what you will learn how to do when you learn and practice the formula, the Model created by Brooke, that I am certified to teach as a graduate of The Life Coach School certification program.

The best part of learning the formula is that once you understand how these two systems operate and how to manage them, nothing is standing in the way of you having the accounting career and the life you want. Remember all those boxes you checked in the introduction? You can begin to uncheck them by learning how to better use your accountant's brain and delineate between System 1 and System 2.

When you can take charge more often and be the Supervising Mother/Father, as opposed to the rambunctious Toddler, that's when you can become a much Smarter Accountant.

Using The Higher Part Of Your Brain More Intentionally

The issue for most, if not all, accountants is what the authors of the book *The 15 Commitments Of Conscious Leadership* refer to as "living below the line". Most accountants let System 1, their lower Toddler brain, run the show more than 80% of the time without being aware that they're doing it.

They unknowingly let System 1 dictate things, creating an unmanageable life. When you are living below the line, you are letting the Toddler decide for you.

I don't know about you, but the last thing I want is a Toddler running my career or my life. Unfortunately, that's exactly what most accountants are unknowingly doing, and it's also where their tendency to argue for their limitations comes from.

To be a Smarter Accountant, you need to learn how to start "living above the line". You need to start using System 2, the higher part of your human brain, the Supervising Mother/Father, more often and more intentionally.

To do this, I'm going to share the formula (i.e., The Model). I'll be describing this in more detail but suffice it to say that this formula that will make you a Smarter Accountant will simply come down to learning how to manage your mind.

You'll be learning this awareness tool to work on anything that you're struggling with, anything you'd like to improve, or any goal you have. The Model will show you why those boxes are currently checked and more importantly, how to uncheck them.

The only thing you need to know to work with The Model is one of 5 things - what's the situation, what are you thinking, what you are feeling, what you are doing or not doing, or what results you currently have. That's it.

For example - what's happening at work? What do you think about tax season? How do you feel about the recent Tax Code changes?

Are you getting more work done in less time? Are you earning as much as you want? These are just a few questions you will be asking yourself as I show you how to be a Smarter Accountant.

Before We Move On

As my accounting clients have discovered, learning to manage your mind is a process, but well worth the time to learn this important skill. With a managed mind, becoming a Smarter Accountant is not only possible but inevitable.

The truth is that your brain is the most important asset an accountant has; you've just been underutilizing yours. I will teach you The Model, but as you already know, learning something is one thing; implementing it is another.

This is why I have created The Smarter Accountant Coaching Program. It's where I can personally coach you and guide you on your way to becoming a Smarter Accountant (you can find out more at www.thesmarteraccountant.com).

Once you have a clearer picture of your unique accountant brain, you can use the formula of The Model to take back control. Now let me explain The Model.

CHAPTER THREE: THE MODEL

Barbara's Story

Barbara is a dedicated accountant and a mom. She asked to work with me just before tax season started, in the midst of COVID-related restrictions and all the changes that affected the small accounting firm she worked for. She was working from home but having a difficult time managing her time, her boss' requests, her family, and everything else she had on her plate, including her health concerns.

Like many people during that time, she felt that so many things weren't within her control and that she was drowning in overwhelm. As is the case with many of my coaching clients, she initially came to me on the verge of burnout, believing that maybe the accounting profession wasn't for her; that there were just too many things weighing on her, especially when it related to her time management and being as productive and efficient as she could be.

Just a few weeks into our weekly coaching sessions, she could see much more clearly how much control she had. She was learning how to manage her time by learning the most important step that no one teaches you in any accounting course CPE seminar - when you learn how to manage your mind, you can manage everything else.

desired R's

She began to delineate between what was a circumstance and what was a thought (I'll explain more in this chapter), allowing her to get more done in less time, manage the expectations of her boss, set boundaries when she needed to, reduce her level of stress, and take back control of what seemed to be out of control.

By learning and applying The Model to things like her schedule, workload, relationships, and stress, she could see improvements that just kept building. As we continued to work together to create the results she wanted, things became clearer and more manageable.

The more she applied The Model, the more she felt in control. The more control she had, the Smarter Accountant she became.

The Power Of The Model For Accountants

As I shared earlier, when I learned the Self Coaching Model created by Brooke Castillo of The Life Coach School, everything changed for me. My relationships, my health, my finances, and my level of stress - all improved once I learned how to use the Self Coaching Model.

But the biggest game-changer was applying it professionally. Having been a CPA in public accounting for almost 30 years at the time, it seemed like too big of a leap to apply what was getting me amazing results in my personal life to my professional life as well.

Like most accountants, I used to believe things like tax season is *[common T's]* stressful, having too much work creates overwhelm, and it's challenging to have difficult clients. I worked with and went to training seminars with other accountants that believed the same things.

However, once I started working with and applying Brooke's Self Coaching Model and saw the changes that the work was having on my accounting career, I knew every accountant needed to know this as well. I could clearly see why accountants were doomed to experience burnout and why so many were struggling both personally and professionally.

As I began to document the incredible before and after effects of learning how to manage my own accountant brain, I finally understood how much power I had to create the accounting career I wanted. I now understood that all the "normal" beliefs accountants have are optional, and I proved it to myself by using The Model to challenge them all.

Having been a CPA in public accounting for so long, I had a lot of beliefs about being an accountant and the profession of accounting that I was open and willing to look at and question. Like you, I knew WHAT I wanted in my life, but I just didn't know HOW - The Model showed me how.

The interesting thing I learned is that our brain has a filter that shows us proof of our beliefs. It's the reason why, for example, if you've ever been in the market for a particular car, say a red Toyota Camry, you will then begin seeing that car all over the road.

That is your brain's amazing ability to process millions of bits of data and show you what you've deemed important based on what you repetitively think about. This amazing filter is great when you don't want to be overwhelmed with those millions of bits of data, but it's not so great if you're an accountant that's feeling overwhelmed and burned out.

The reason it's not beneficial is that your practiced beliefs, and those of other accountants that you work with or speak to, then become the filter that your accountant's brain uses. Until you challenge those beliefs, your brain will keep showing you the same red Toyota Camry.

Until I was willing to challenge the practiced beliefs of our accounting profession, I believed what everyone else believed. That was until I discovered the formula.

Thankfully, I'm not a special snowflake. I can show you the formula so that you can have the opportunity to have the same results that I, and my clients, have had.

What Is The Model?

The Model is a formula that consists of 5 parts:

1. Circumstance
2. Thought
3. Feeling
4. Actions
5. Result

It seems simple, right? Don't be fooled by its simplicity because this formula will bust those myths you have about what's "normal," and will help you become a Smarter Accountant in the process.

The Model is like a magnifying glass that helps us to see what's going on with us; why we feel how we feel, why we do or don't do certain things, and why we have the results we have in a different way than we usually do.

The #1 reason we do Models is to become more aware of what's happening with us and to understand what we have control over. The Model is not only an awareness tool, but it's also a formula to help you understand everything about your life and how to uncheck those boxes you checked in the Introduction.

Like any formula, it helps you see the components that lead to a particular result. It gives you so much information and perspective.

The Model allows you to take a birds' eye view of what's happening in your life, as opposed to feeling like you have no control. It helps you live intentionally instead of being a victim of your circumstances.

Once you work with The Model, you can start choosing your life intentionally. You can see the components of the equation that give you an *unin*tentional result and the components of the equation that can give you an *in*tentional result.

So now, let me explain each of the 5 parts a little more in-depth.

Circumstance

A circumstance is all the people, places, and things in your life. The most important thing to know about circumstances is that **they are all neutral**. When filling in your Model (we'll go over that later), the circumstance line of The Model must be specific and "facty."

You want it to be boring and something that everyone on the planet would agree with or that you could prove in a court of law. Circumstances do not contain adjectives, opinions, or thoughts.

It's incredibly important to ensure that your circumstance line of the formula is neutral because we often believe that we're stating a *fact* when we are really stating a *thought*. You'll see the importance and the power of delineating between the two when you work on creating a Model.

One of the most amazing things about using this formula is that just having the clarity between a circumstance versus a thought about a circumstance can make a huge difference. For example, you might believe it's a fact that your mother-in-law is difficult, but that's actually a thought. The circumstance would be "I have a mother-in-law named (fill in the blank)."

Once you start to work with The Model, you'll see why this matters, but for now, just know that circumstances are the things you have no control over. The good news is that everything else in the formula you DO have control over.

Thought

Thoughts are the sentences or phrases you have in your brain about the circumstances in your life. The key to becoming a Smarter Accountant is understanding two very important things - that your thoughts are optional and that they create your feelings. No exceptions!

You might want to argue that the thoughts and beliefs you have about various things in your life are true, but they're optional. One of the most powerful questions you can ask yourself is, "It might seem true, but is it helpful?"

The truth is that we all have a lot of thoughts about the people, places, and things in our lives, but we rarely take the time to stop and question whether our thoughts are serving us. Ironically, we'll often defend our right to believe something that isn't helpful at all.

As you work with The Model, you'll begin to see how your thoughts are the pivotal piece of the formula for being a Smarter Accountant. Like most people, you can most likely look at one circumstance and have many thoughts about it, but the most important thing I work on with my clients is creating awareness around how to delineate a circumstance from a thought.

The power of this formula is that while circumstances are typically NOT in your control, your thoughts ARE. While you can't change most circumstances in your life, you can choose what you think about them.

For example:

- **Circumstance:** Joe completed 2 out of 6 tax returns

- **Thought:** Joe isn't working hard enough

- **Circumstance:** My daughter is 12 years old

- **Thought:** My daughter is too young to be going to the movies alone with friends

- **Circumstance:** I am driving my car at 20 mph

- **Thought:** This traffic is ridiculous

The most important thing to know when it comes to thoughts is that your thoughts create your feelings, not the other way around. For example, you don't think "Joe isn't working hard enough" because you feel frustrated; you create the feeling of frustration from the thought "Joe isn't working hard enough."

This might seem like semantics, but I promise you it's not. To become a Smarter Accountant, you have to understand that your brain offers you thoughts about circumstances, and those thoughts create your feelings.

Feeling

In The Model, your feelings are the one-word emotions created by your thoughts. You feel sad, mad, stressed, happy, excited, etc., because you have a thought that precedes the feeling.

For many accountants, feelings are swept under the rug or are believed to have no place in business. The issue is that how you feel is WAY more important than you realize, for one key reason - how you feel determines what you do or don't do.

If you want to be more productive and efficient, get more done in less time, close that sale, or improve your relationship with your children, you need to get clear about your feelings. How you currently feel and how you would like to feel are all dictated by the second line in the formula - the thought line.

For example:

Circumstance: Joe completed 2 out of 6 tax returns

Thought: Joe isn't working hard enough

Feeling: Frustrated

Notice how the circumstance is neutral - the fact is that Joe completed 2 out of 6 tax returns. But here's the key - that circumstance doesn't mean anything until you have a thought about it, and it's that thought that creates the feeling of frustrated, not the fact that Joe completed 2 out of 6 tax returns.

Most accountants would argue that they feel frustrated because of the circumstance, but that is never the reason. The only reason you would feel frustrated is that your lower brain offered you the thought, "Joe isn't working hard enough."

So, what does this have to do with being a Smarter Accountant? Because just like the thought line creates the feeling line, the feeling line then creates the next line in the formula - the action line.

Once you work with The Model, choosing how you want to feel on purpose, instead of leaving it up to the Toddler part of your brain, the more you'll see how much control you actually have and how to become a Smarter Accountant.

You don't need to take more CPE courses to make you smarter. You need to clarify how The Model formula plays out in your work and your life and then what to do about it.

Actions

This fourth line in The Model represents the things you do and the things you don't do, as well as your reactions. This is where you describe all of your actions and inactions; the things we could see if we were a fly on the wall, and the things swirling around in your brain.

Interestingly, this is where most accountants put their focus. Most of us gravitated to accounting because we like solving problems, so we tend to put most of our attention on taking action.

Unfortunately, we tend to do an awful lot yet still check so many of those boxes that you checked in the introduction. So, if you're always so busy and you take a lot of action, then what's the problem? Why are so many accountants on the verge of burnout?

The answer is that focusing on the action line without first getting clear on the thought and feeling lines of The Model leads to ineffective action. It also leads to busyness for the sake of being busy; a complete misuse of your time.

No matter what the actions are, you have to question the thought and the feeling that is fueling those actions. The way I describe it to my coaching clients is that your feelings are like the fuel you use to take actions; make sure you're using the best and cleanest fuel you can.

For example:

Circumstance: Joe completed 2 out of 6 tax returns

Thought: Joe isn't working hard enough

Feeling: Frustrated

Actions: Complain about Joe; micro-manage him; look for other ways he isn't working hard enough; don't give him the benefit of the doubt; don't check in with him

From the "dirty fuel" of the feeling of frustration, the actions you take or don't take, as well as your reaction to the uncomfortability of frustration, will lead you to take ineffective actions. To be a Smarter Accountant, you have to look at your feelings as information, not problems, and choose the best feeling for the best actions.

Your actions are so important because they will ultimately create your results. The things you do, the things you don't do, and your reactions, will always create the results you end up with.

Result

The final line of The Model is your results, or the effect of everything that you thought, felt and did. The interesting thing about your results is that they will always be proof for your thoughts.

As you'll see throughout this book, your thought line always ends up in your results line based on how you feel and the actions you take or don't take. In essence, you prove your thoughts by the Thought -> Feeling -> Action cycle.

For example:

Circumstance: Joe completed 2 out of 6 tax returns

Thought: Joe isn't working hard enough

Feeling: Frustrated

Actions: Complain about Joe; micro-manage him; look for other ways he isn't working hard enough; get distracted from my own work; focus more on Joe than on myself; don't give him the benefit of the doubt; don't check in with him

Result: I'm not working hard enough

Notice how the thought "Joe isn't working hard enough" ultimately ends up with me not working hard enough based on the feeling of frustration and what I did and didn't do from that feeling. The power of The Model is being able to clearly see why you have the results you have.

Interestingly, most of us just believe life happens TO us. We're unhappy with our finances, lack of work/life balance, health, or relationships, and we just think there's nothing we can do about it.

We're taught to believe certain things by our families, our society, and our peers, never thinking to question whether those thoughts and beliefs are serving us or not. If you want to know if they're serving you, just look at how many boxes you checked in the Introduction.

The truth is that to become a Smarter Accountant, you need to be open to the formula that I've shared and use it to create better results than you currently have. Most of us believe that there are things we don't have any control over, but here's the *most* important thing I want you to get from this book - *the only line in The Model that you DON'T have control over is the circumstance line.*

That's right; *everything* below the circumstance line *is* within your control, but you were just never taught that it was. Being a Smarter Accountant means knowing that circumstances are neutral and that you have the power to not only think, feel, and act in a way that serves you but that you can also create the results you really want.

So, there you have it - the 5-part formula for The Model. As with everything, knowing it is great; using it is even better!

Before We Move On

One of the most important things to know about The Model is that this is an awareness tool. I'll be sharing some other tools throughout the book, but in order to be a Smarter Accountant, you must begin to create more awareness of the thoughts that are actually creating the results you have, both professionally and personally.

You already know that you're typically one of the smartest people in the room, but The Model is the secret to being even smarter. The hard truth is that if you checked any of those boxes in the Introduction, you're not being as smart as you could be. It might be hard to hear, but it's true.

I'm not trying to be judgmental; I'm just trying to give you a wake-up call. All those limiting beliefs that most accountants have about how difficult things are and how it's just the way it is are optional.

As you become a Smarter Accountant, you will get excited by the fact that if something is an optional thought, you get to choose a more helpful thought. Again, the only thing that is not in your control is the circumstance line of The Model - everything else is optional.

Thankfully, becoming a Smarter Accountant doesn't have to take a lot of time if you get support and guidance from The Smarter Accountant Coaching Program. Like most accountants, you've been allowing the Toddler part of your brain to run the show for way too long; it's time to take charge and be that Supervising Mother/Father in order to have the accounting career and the life you want.

To answer the question *"If I'm so smart, why (fill in the blank)?"* you have to be willing to challenge those limiting beliefs and train your accountant brain in order to be a Smarter Accountant. The good news is that you're already smart, but I can show you how to be smarter.

In Part II, each of those boxes you checked in the Introduction will be addressed, helping you become a much Smarter Accountant. You'll be able to see The Model in action.

Hopefully, what you'll notice is that you can apply The Model to *ANYTHING*, not just those checked boxes. Once you learn how to be a Smarter Accountant, no matter the circumstance, you'll know exactly what to do to get the desired result.

I can't wait for you to apply this formula to not only your work but to your finances, your health, your relationships, and any goal you'd like to achieve. As I shared before, learning the formula of The Model will not only help you be a Smarter Accountant, but it will also help you be a smarter woman, man, mother, father, friend, etc.

Without further ado, let's jump into getting those boxes unchecked!!

PART II—UNCHECKING THE BOXES

CHAPTER ONE: INTRODUCTION

Hopefully, now that you've read Part One and understand that you've been underusing your brain, the second half of this book is going to offer examples of how to become a Smarter Accountant, and how you can use the Model to uncheck the boxes you checked in the Introduction in Part One. This is where you can see the model in action as well as how to apply it to any challenge you're experiencing, either professionally or personally.

No matter which boxes you checked or didn't check, I suggest you read through each of the following chapters for two simple reasons —first, your accountant's life is always going to change and evolve, and, second, you're taking your accountant brain with you. As you've probably already experienced, just when you've unchecked one box and understand how to handle a particular situation, another one pops up that you may not have dealt with before.

Also, the reason why I suggest you read each of the following chapters is that, as I mentioned in Part One, I will be sharing additional tools and helpful tips. The Model is the most powerful tool I use when working with my coaching clients but there's also more that you'll want to know as well.

The beauty of becoming a Smarter Accountant and truly understanding the power of the formula I discussed in Part One is that—no matter what happens—you'll be able to handle it. There is no reason for you to feel powerless any longer or, like a lot of accountants I hear from, to grapple with issues such as whether you even want to stay in the accounting profession.

When you become a Smarter Accountant, you will be able to see things differently as well as to have options that you might not have considered before. You'll also be able to experience less stress, overwhelm, and confusion, and to begin enjoying much more clarity, confidence, and control.

There's no question that you're already smart or you wouldn't be in the accounting profession. The issue is that—because you're smart—you think that what you believe is a fact.

For example, if you feel stressed and overwhelmed when you work too many hours, or you just can't figure out how to create more hours in the day, you think that there cannot be an answer to the problems you're faced with or you would have figured out the solution already (or at least some other smart accountant would have?). Well, congratulations because I am that SMARTER Accountant and I hope you will become one as well!

The only difference between you and me is that I was willing to question all those beliefs that accountants assume are facts, learn how our accountant's brain works and how to manage it, and do the work to uncheck all the boxes. I figured it out so that I can now help you become a Smarter Accountant as well. I hope that you will not only achieve this but that you'll also share this book with others. This is the opportunity for us, and future generations of accountants, to become empowered so that we have much more control over our future careers and lives.

This is the opportunity for us to learn how to do things differently, make changes in our lives, and not succumb to burnout. It's the chance to change the trajectory of our profession so that generations come to see accounting as a rewarding path rather than a soul-sucking career.

I hope you see me as an example of what's possible when you learn how to manage your accountant's brain. So, if you're ready to get the answer to the question, "If I'm so smart, why...?", then let's begin!

Warning: Before I explain how to uncheck any of the boxes from the Introduction to Part One, I strongly suggest that you read Part One first (if you haven't already). In that first part, I explain the basics of the formula, the Manage Your Mind Model. You cannot uncheck any of the boxes without understanding the Model first.

CHAPTER TWO: IF I'M SO SMART, WHY DO I FEEL SO STRESSED AND OVERWHELMED, ESPECIALLY DURING DEADLINES?

Mary's Story

Mary was feeling completely overwhelmed with her accounting practice. She had left the mid-sized public accounting firm she had worked at for 10 years and was looking forward to being her own boss.

The issue wasn't that Mary had difficulty getting clients: it was that she not only had too many clients, but she also didn't know how to say "No". Her life was completely out of balance.

When she was asked what her three most common daily feelings were, her response was "Stress, overwhelm, and doubt". It didn't matter who asked—her response was typically at least one of those three, and often a combination of them all.

Mary especially felt those three emotions when deadlines were looming, like the tax season or the quarterly financial requirements for some of her clients. Her levels of stress and overwhelm weren't just affecting her work, they were affecting other areas of her life as well.

She had gone out on her own to have less stress and to be able to spend more time with her two children but, unfortunately, she realized that she had more stress now than when she worked for her former firm. She even considered going back to the firm but quickly remembered that she had felt those same three feelings there as well.

Additionally, being a single mom and wanting to start dating again, she also recognized that her levels of stress and overwhelm were making her plans for the future difficult. She carried those feelings around like a heavy purse, not knowing what to do about them.

She spoke to other accountant solopreneurs who felt the same way, ultimately leading her to resign herself to the belief that this must be how it was going to be. She didn't like it but she also didn't believe that she had any other option.

Many times throughout the years, she asked herself, "If I'm so smart, why am I so stressed and overwhelmed?"

The Truth About Stress and Overwhelm

If you can relate to Mary's story, the best news that I can give you is that the Model holds the answer. The hard truth is that your smart accountant brain is being underused.

How do I know? Because you wouldn't feel so much stress and overwhelm if you were using the higher, prefrontal cortex part of your brain more intentionally and more often.

Remember what I shared in Part One about System 1 (aka the Toddler) versus System 2 (aka the Supervising Mother/Father)? The reason you feel stressed and overwhelmed, especially during times of deadlines, is because you're letting the Toddler, the default part of your brain, run the show.

When you don't manage your accountant's brain, you end up day after day, year after year, feeling stressed and overwhelmed, often ending in burnout. Thankfully though, you were smart enough to buy this book—you were smart enough to want to become a Smarter Accountant.

I promise you that by better understanding the truth behind my stress and overwhelm, especially as an accountant in public accounting, I have changed everything in my life for the better. I cannot emphasize this enough—stress and overwhelm are OPTIONAL for accountants!

How is that possible? Let me show you how.

Unchecking the Box

So how can it be that stress and overwhelm are optional? Because the Model shows you that, although you don't necessarily have control over circumstances, everything below the circumstance line in the Model is optional.

If you're thinking, "I still don't get how stress and overwhelm are optional?", here's why—because they are feelings.

The reason this is so important, when it comes to the formula of the Model, is that a feeling is the third line of the Model. And what comes before a feeling in the Model? A thought.

Unfortunately, every single accountant I speak to (*who hasn't been coached by me*) believes that circumstances cause feelings. They wouldn't necessarily say it that way, but that's what they believe.

For example, ask any accountant in public accounting if the tax season is difficult and stressful, and most, if not all, will say "Yes!" But that's only because they don't know the Model and they haven't been coached by me.

To be a Smarter Accountant, you have to understand that circumstances don't cause feelings. A Smarter Accountant knows that feelings are caused by the optional thoughts their default brain has about circumstances.

The truth is that the tax season is just dates on the calendar: it's a block of time. Remember what I explained in Part One—a circumstance, like dates on a calendar, cannot create the feeling of stress or overwhelm.

The only thing that CAN cause those feelings is a thought about the circumstance. The only thing that is causing you stress and overwhelm is your unmanaged brain's thoughts about circumstances like the dates on the calendar, the number of tax returns that need to be filed, etc.

Your unmanaged accountant brain is the issue, not dates on the calendar, the amount of work you have to get done, the expectations of your clients, etc. To understand this better, let me show you an example.

Here's what a typical Model looks like for an unmanaged accountant:

Circumstance: Today is April 1st

Thought: Tax season is too hard

Feeling: Stressed

Actions: Struggle to get a handle on the workload; spin in confusion about what to do next; procrastinate; avoid client emails; snap at kids when I'm home; not present with family; eat more than usual to feel better; don't sleep well; dread going to work

Result: I make it too hard on me

As you can see, the feeling of stress fueled actions, inactions, and reactions that culminated in this accountant making the tax season too hard on them personally. The problem wasn't the date on the calendar—it was their thoughts about the date on the calendar.

Here's what a Model looks like for a Smarter Accountant:

Circumstance: Today is April 1st

Thought: This doesn't have to be so hard

Feeling: Focused

Actions: Put together a plan for getting everything done in the next 2 weeks; calendar my time to make sure I'm using it wisely; plan "Focus Time" at my optimal time; schedule 1 hour a day to answer client emails; turn off all notifications on phone and computer; spend quality time with family when I'm home; pay attention to what I'm eating and drinking; get to bed early and wake up early; look forward to a productive day at work

Result: I make it easier for me

By choosing the feeling of focused, on purpose, and then choosing a believable thought to put into the Model, this accountant would be able to take much more productive action. By choosing the thought "This doesn't have to be so hard", their actions would create a better result—personally experiencing April 1st as not so hard.

It's important to note that the unmanaged accountant most likely blamed the fact that "today is April 1st" for their feeling of stress, but the Smarter Accountant knows better. The Smarter Accountant knows that stress is only ever created by an optional thought and that stress is one of the "dirtiest fuels" to use to take productive action.

The Smarter Accountant recognizes that stress is optional and they stop blaming circumstances. They understand that they have control over their results and they don't let their Toddler brain take control.

Summary

The beauty in becoming a Smarter Accountant is that you don't need any circumstance to be different in order to feel better or have a better result. The solution to feeling stressed and overwhelmed, especially during deadlines, is to intentionally choose how you want to feel.

The truth is that the default part of your brain, the Toddler, is so used to thinking certain limiting beliefs that you couldn't possibly do anything about it. Until now!

When I work with my coaching clients in the Smarter Accountant Program, we focus on uncovering all those limiting beliefs that most accountants have, and then on becoming a Smarter Accountant. The key is understanding that your accountant's brain has over 60,000 thoughts a day—60,000!

This is why it's so important to learn how to have more awareness when it comes to what's creating the results you currently have. The reason you have those results is because of the second line of the Model—a Thought.

As I previously shared, your thought line will always end up in your result line. The truth is that your thoughts create your feelings, your feelings fuel your actions, and your actions create your results. Every time.

That is why, if you want to be a Smarter Accountant, you must begin to be more aware of your thoughts. Unless you want to keep creating the same results, you have to pay attention to what you're thinking.

The tool we use in the Smarter Accountant Program is called a "Thought Download", whereby my clients learn how to empty some of those 60,000 thoughts onto paper. Remember, the most amazing thing about the human brain is that we get to think about what we think about.

If you want to become a Smarter Accountant, you have to learn how to take a non-judgmental look at what you're thinking. If you want to uncheck that box and stop feeling so stressed and overwhelmed, you have to understand your unique brain better and how to manage it.

When you become a Smarter Accountant, you'll finally see that stress and overwhelm are optional. You'll begin to create the awareness of what is causing you to feel stressed and overwhelmed (remember, it's not caused by circumstances), and you'll know how to change those unhelpful feelings to ones that get you the results you want.

So the answer to the question, "If I'm so smart, why do I feel so stressed and overwhelmed, especially during deadlines?" is because you haven't learned how to manage your accountant's brain, yet.

CHAPTER THREE: IF I'M SO SMART, WHY DO I WORK TOO MANY HOURS?

Joe's Story

Joe was a CPA who had worked his way up to senior manager at his firm. He was the first person in his family to graduate from college and he wanted to make his extended family proud.

It wasn't easy, but he was determined to grow professionally. He was well respected at the firm and often the one who stayed the latest at the office, working many more hours than his colleagues.

The building's maintenance team who came to straighten up after hours often joked about how there was no way that Joe had a wife at home. He worked too many hours for any woman to stay happily married to him.

The problem was that Joe did have a wife and two young children at home.

When he first got married, his wife was very understanding of the pressure he was under to pass the CPA exam and the steps he felt he needed to take to move up in his career. But once they started having children, she became frustrated with Joe's late hours.

He was missing so much time with their children—time he would never be able to get back. He was missing time with his wife as well and their relationship was suffering.

Although they discussed him not working so many hours, he just couldn't figure out how to not only slow down but also how to still get all his work done. It felt like a Catch-22: the more hours he worked, the more anxious he felt; the more anxious he felt, the less efficient he was; the less efficient he was, the more hours he needed to work.

Even though he was only in his late 30s, his health was suffering as well. He wasn't eating properly because he was never home for a healthy, home-cooked meal, he wasn't going to the gym like he used to, and he was experiencing sleep problems as well.

The real issue was that Joe was secretly using work as a way to try to build his lack of self-confidence. A large part of the reason why he was working too many hours was that he was trying to prove his worth—to the firm, to his family, and himself.

Many times, as he worked late in the office after everyone else had left, he asked himself, "If I'm so smart, why am I working too many hours?"

The Truth About Working Too Many Hours

If you can relate to Joe's story, you're in luck! One of the many benefits of becoming a Smarter Accountant is the ability to address an issue that plagues so many accountants—working too many hours.

If you checked this box in the Introduction to Part One, you most likely have a family or others in your life who are also being affected by all those work hours. And, just like Joe, I'm going to bet you are also being detrimentally affected in many ways, possibly including your relationships, your health, and your happiness.

While working too many hours has various causes, such as fear, anxiety, a scarcity mindset, a lack of time management skills, and a propensity to overcommit, the one main cause that I see the most when I'm coaching clients is a lack of self-confidence. Hands down, this is one of the most common issues for many accountants.

Even with all the advanced knowledge and degrees, the letters after our last names, and the continuing professional education, accountants tend to have an issue with self-confidence. It's a large part of the reason why we feel the need to go after those degrees and those extra letters after our last names—we believe those accomplishments and accolades will make us feel confident.

Here's the other tricky thing when it comes to working too many hours—it's also highly encouraged by the accounting profession. If you think about it, overeating, overdrinking, and overspending are frowned upon by society but when it comes to overworking, especially for accountants, this is rarely met with concern for the accountant's overall well-being.

If we're being completely honest, as accountants, we tend to judge each other based on how many hours we work. For example, I was once walking in the hallway of my office building when I passed two accountants from another office in the building. One said to the other, "Did you see that Larry's car wasn't in the parking lot last night?" to which the other accountant replied, "He must not be very good at what he does."

This badge of honor that has become the norm in the accounting profession might be considered good for business but it's also leading to more marital, parenting, health, and burnout issues than anything else. But what's an accountant supposed to do if they struggle with working too many hours?

Thankfully, once again, the Model has the answer! It can show you WHY, for example, you don't feel confident and it can also show you HOW to improve your self-confidence.

I might sound like a broken record but I will continue to point this out to you throughout this book—if you were using the higher part of your brain more intentionally, you wouldn't be working too many hours. It's that simple.

When you don't manage your accountant brain better, it's easy to believe that hard work equates to your worth and will create self-confidence. But, as the adage suggests, "Work smarter, not harder" —thankfully, becoming a Smarter Accountant will help you uncheck the box of working too many hours.

How is that possible? Let me show you how.

Unchecking the Box

So how is it possible to not work too many hours and still be successful as an accountant? Because the Model shows you that the reason you're taking the action of overworking is because of a feeling.

Remember, your actions, reactions, and inactions are all fueled by your feelings. When you uncover the feeling driving your actions, you'll understand why you're working too many hours.

When I work with my coaching clients in the Smarter Accountant Program, awareness is everything. At first, it can be challenging for them to uncover the feeling behind what's driving them to overwork but, as I shared before, this typically comes from a lack of confidence.

In Joe's example, he secretly had an issue with self-confidence, believing that his worth was dependent on how many hours he worked. The problem was that he didn't know that you CAN NOT take action to create a feeling—your feelings always precede your actions.

This is why Smarter Accountants truly understand how to work smarter, not harder. They're not trying to create a feeling of confidence, or create any better feeling, by taking action—they're creating confidence by the optional thoughts they're choosing on purpose and then taking action.

Again, to be a Smarter Accountant, you have to understand that actions don't cause feelings. A Smarter Accountant knows that not only do feelings fuel actions but that they also get much more done in less time when they choose better feelings to fuel their actions.

I also want to point out that all those credentials, higher education, and letters after your last name are just neutral circumstances in the Model. They actually cannot create a feeling of confidence, or any other feeling, no matter how hard you try to make the connection.

The only thing that CAN cause a feeling of confidence is a thought—specifically a thought about you. Therefore, the only thing that is causing you to NOT feel confident is your unmanaged brain's thoughts about you.

Your unmanaged accountant brain is the issue, not you. To understand this better, let me show you an example.

Here's what a typical Model looks like for an unmanaged accountant:

Circumstance: Quarterly financials for XYZ client due in 2 weeks

Thought: I don't see how I'm ever going to get this done

Feeling: Self-doubt

Actions: Complain about the project; tell myself I should be better than I am; struggle with imposter syndrome; procrastinate; beat myself up; spin in self-judgment; question whether I have what it takes; spend time indulging in confusion; work too many hours; don't create a plan of action; don't look for all the ways I am capable; don't get rest in order to be at my best

Result: I don't get it done

As you can see, the actions, including working too many hours, were fueled by the feeling of self-doubt. But the key here is that it wasn't the quarterly financials for the XYZ client that were due in 2 weeks that created the feeling of self-doubt—it was the thought, "I don't see how I'm ever going to get this done" that created the feeling of self-doubt.

Here's what a Model looks like for a Smarter Accountant:

Circumstance: Quarterly financials for XYZ client due in 2 weeks

Thought: I will finish this without working too many hours

Feeling: Self-confidence

Actions: Put together a to-do list with a timeline; calendar everything that needs to be done; schedule uninterrupted Focus Time each day when all notifications are turned off; make sure I pack healthy food to bring to work to keep my energy up; reschedule unimportant meetings; ask for help when needed; get clear about how to get everything done without working extra hours; remind myself how capable I am; get plenty of rest

Result: I finish this project without working too many hours

The Smarter Accountant didn't wait for the feeling of self-confidence, they created it by choosing a much more helpful thought. By choosing the thought, "I will finish this without working too many hours", they created the feeling of self-confidence on purpose and their actions created the result that proved their thought—they finished the project without working too many hours.

When I work with my coaching clients, even if we discover that the reason they were working too many hours was fueled by a feeling other than self-doubt, they are still able to take back control. The Model always shows you what's behind your issue.

The clients who have had this issue for a while are amazed at how much more they're able to get done in less time, how much better they feel about themselves, and how much other areas of their life improve just by becoming a Smarter Accountant.

Summary

One of the best parts about becoming a Smarter Accountant is the fact that it becomes much easier to figure out how to have the career and the life that you want. You no longer have to be at the mercy of norms such as the accounting profession's tendency to exist on the brink of burnout.

As I previously explained, not knowing how your unique accountant brain works is like having the most amazing piece of machinery on the planet and never reading the instruction manual. I not only help my coaching clients understand their brain's instruction manual; I also help them fine-tune the advanced features as well.

Another important thing to understand with an issue like working too many hours is the concept of buffering. "Buffering" is a term used to describe the actions we take to lessen or moderate the impact of something, which results in a net negative effect.

For example, you feel anxious, so you buffer by having a few drinks at the end of the day. Unfortunately, you don't get the rest you need, you wake up not feeling your best, and you can't focus like you would with a clear head.

The interesting thing is that, as science expands in its understanding of the human brain, we now know that over the millennia the lower, primitive brain has been motivated by three things—to avoid pain, seek pleasure, and be efficient. When we seek pleasure, our brains release a chemical called dopamine, which gives us a momentary feeling of relief.

Therefore, when we use buffering in our lives, it's to lessen the impact of our negative emotions, with overworking being one of the buffering activities that I have found most common in accountants. The issue is that while we say we want happy, authentic, balanced lives, we wind up using things like food, social media, and work to give us false pleasure.

Another thing I see with my coaching clients is being a "work martyr" (more on this in Chapter Twelve). Work martyrdom can show up in various ways, like taking work home so that you can get a jump-start on everyone else, not taking all your paid time off because you're afraid it will look bad, or not being able to delegate because you're worried that no one else can do the work as well as you.

Work martyrdom can also be sneaky because it's often perceived to be normal, necessary or, even worse, rewarded. Thankfully, being a Smarter Accountant means being able to drop the thorny crown of work martyrdom and instead to have the professional and personal life you truly desire.

If you want to be a Smarter Accountant, you need to stop using things like work to make you feel confident and worthy. If you want to uncheck that box and stop working too many hours, you have to understand your unique brain better and how to manage it.

CHAPTER FOUR: IF I'M SO SMART, WHY IS MY LIFE SO UNBALANCED AND MY TIME MANAGEMENT SUCH AN ISSUE?

Lisa's Story

Lisa was a CPA in public accounting and, like many other accountants, on the verge of burnout. She was working a minimum of 60–70 hours per week (more during the tax season) but wasn't able to see any other way to advance.

She was committed to both her career and her family but felt that, to have career success, she needed to give up the idea of a balanced life. Every time she thought she had a better handle on her time management and had some semblance of balance, it all seemed to get turned upside down.

Just when she thought she had some control over her time, her husband's job would demand more of his time, her two children would want to get involved in various sports, her widowed mother would need more support, and her friends would start to get annoyed by her lack of involvement with them. It got to the point where she wasn't sure she would ever be able to have a successful career and a balanced life.

Her daily thoughts were:

- What I'm willing to give is not enough.
- Nothing I do will ever be enough.

- I can't do more—I have kids.
- To be successful in my career, I will have to sacrifice the other parts of my life.
- If I choose a balanced life, I'll never be successful.
- I can't be all-in at work without giving up my life outside of work.
- The kids won't want to snuggle you forever.
- They're only little for a short time.
- They'll be big in a blink of an eye and I'll have missed it.
- I'm trying so hard but not getting any credit for the effort I am putting in.
- There's just too much to learn and too much to do.
- I don't have enough time and energy to do it all.

What Lisa was struggling with was not how to manage her career and her family—she was struggling with an unmanaged mind. Until she learned THAT skill, she would slowly burn out over time.

Many times, as she drove home from work, well past the time she wanted to leave the office, she asked herself, "If I'm so smart, why is my life so unbalanced and my time management such an issue?"

The Truth About Balance and Time Management

If balance and time management are issues for you, I can help—it's one of my specialties! One of the many benefits of my doing the work to become a Smarter Accountant is that I have also cracked the code on time management for accountants.

In essence (to paraphrase from *Star Trek*), I've "boldly been able to go where no accountant has gone before"—I've been able to figure out the cause of the problem that most accountants experience with balance and time management. Ever since I have learned, tested, and succeeded at better time management, it has been one of my greatest pleasures to be able to coach accountants to show them the secret.

But here's where some tough love needs to happen when it comes to accountants and time management: time is NOT the problem—you are. In other words, time doesn't need to be managed—your brain does.

The truth about balance and time management is that most accountants have a lot of "time drama", a term I coined to describe the mental drama you experience around anything having to do with how you do or don't use your time. It's one of the main reasons why you checked the box in the Introduction to Part One about having an unbalanced life and struggling with time management.

It's important to have this awareness because time drama is what most accountants experience in their relationship with time. Unfortunately, if you're not aware of it, time drama can derail you before you know what's happening. It often sounds like the following:

- This is too hard.

- I can't do it.

- There isn't enough time.

- There aren't enough hours in the day.

- I'm just exhausted.

- Tax season is too much.

- Everyone else is stressed about time.

- There's nothing I can do about it.

The funny thing about time drama is that most accountants will argue that they're not being dramatic: they're being truthful. They truly believe that time is the problem. However, that sneaky belief is one of the best ways to spot time drama because—again—time is NOT the problem: your thoughts about time ARE.

It is possible to create balance, to create more hours in the day, and to get more done in less time, freeing you up to have more time for the things and the people you love. But, to make that fantasy a reality, you must learn how to manage your mind before you learn how to manage your time.

I promise you that better time management for accountants isn't just about learning a better process—it's about learning how to become a Smarter Accountant and understanding your unique accountant brain. Once you get a better handle on that, you'll be amazed at how much more balance you'll experience and how improved your time management will become.

If you happen to be shaking your head right now, I understand your reluctance to see time differently from how most accountants do but that's part of the problem—what you believe, your brain looks for proof of. If you don't challenge what you believe, you'll never experience what's possible.

If you are stressed, overwhelmed, and anxious about time, time is not the problem—your brain is, and it's adding unnecessary pressure. There's no time management app, special planner, or practice management software program that can truly fix time drama—again, time is not the problem.

Those apps, planners, and programs are just temporary fixes. Thinking that they'll solve your problem is like trying to deal with a leaky faucet by putting towels underneath to catch the water instead of fixing the leak—you have to stop the leak if you want to fix the problem.

Every accountant knows how to put notes on a calendar and how to schedule their time but they don't know how to manage their brains as they manage their time or guarantee they'll follow through. They're being pulled in so many different directions that time just seems to slip by, and—before they know it—their to-do list has grown and there aren't enough hours in the day to get everything done.

This is when being a Smarter Accountant comes into play.

Unchecking the Box

So how is it possible to have a more balanced life and to better manage your time? The Model shows you that the reason why your current situation is one of an unbalanced life is that you're not making decisions with the higher, prefrontal cortex part of your brain.

You're not using the power of the Supervising Mother/Father part of your brain to manage its Toddler part. You're letting your unmanaged mind dictate what you do and don't do, wasting a lot of time and energy in the process.

To be a Smarter Accountant, you have to understand that the time of year, the date on the calendar, the deadline, and the amount of work you have are all neutral circumstances. They don't mean anything until you make them mean something.

Unfortunately, most accountants have so many unhelpful thoughts when it comes to their workload, the time of year, and so many other aspects of what has to get done and how much time they have in which to get it done. And the worst part is: they've got plenty of other accountants who will agree with them.

Thankfully, as a Smarter Accountant, you can master time management because you will understand that managing your mind has to come first. The only reason you have an unbalanced life and your time management is an issue is because of your unmanaged brain.

Here's what a typical Model looks like for an unmanaged accountant:

Circumstance: To-do list—drop kids at school, meeting, conference call, lunch with a client, tax training, review sales tax return, proposal for potential client, pick up dinner, son's baseball game

Thought: I don't know how I can manage this to-do list

Feeling: Overwhelmed

Actions: Complain about the to-do list; tell myself there's no way I can get everything done; worry about being distracted at lunch with client; procrastinate; consider missing son's baseball game; tell myself I'm a horrible parent; spend time indulging in overwhelm; buffer with email; do things that aren't on the to-do list; don't prioritize; don't create a plan of action; don't get organized; don't look for all the ways I can manage it

Result: I don't manage the to-do list

The key here is that it wasn't the to-do list that was the problem—it was the thought, "I don't see how I'm ever going to get this done," that created the feeling of overwhelm. That feeling is never going to drive the action necessary to get things done, to better manage your time, or to have some semblance of balance.

Here's what a Model looks like for a Smarter Accountant:

Circumstance: To-do list—drop kids at school, meeting, conference call, lunch with a client, tax training, review sales tax return, proposal for potential client, pick up dinner, son's baseball game

Thought: I am open to figuring out how to get this all done

Feeling: Curious

Actions: Put to-do list in priority order; decide how long each item will take; calendar everything that needs to be done; get my higher brain on board by asking "How can I get this all done?"; look for solutions rather than problems; be open to delegating; don't procrastinate; don't beat myself up; stay on task; stay organized; follow the calendar no matter what

Result: I figure out how to get this all done

The Smarter Accountant may have noticed they were feeling overwhelmed at first but then chose to feel curious on purpose. By choosing the thought, "I am open to figuring out how to get this all done", they created the feeling of curiosity and their actions created the result that proved their thought—they figured out how to get this all done.

When I work with my coaching clients on better time management in the Smarter Accounting Program, it always comes down to what they're thinking and feeling. As I said before, time is never the issue when it comes to time management—your brain is—and the Model always shows you the problem as well as the solution.

Becoming a Smarter Accountant helps you create more time by getting more done in less time, stop procrastinating, get more control over your time, and have more time for the things and the people you love. The Smarter Accountant understands how to manage their time to create a balanced life.

Summary

I could write an entire book on better time management for accountants, but I'll keep it simple—most accountants are managing their time incorrectly, which has fed into the belief that time is the problem. You cannot go to work every day believing that time is the problem and then expect to have a better sense of control over it.

With this blame mentality, you're doomed to have sloppy time management — sloppy in both thoughts, feelings, and actions. When you make time the problem, guess what result you create for yourself? More problems.

When you allow the lower, Toddler part of your brain to manage your time (which most accountants unconsciously do), it's no wonder that you're unable to create a foolproof system of time management and follow through on your plans. You're once again not reading your brain's instruction manual and using its helpful features.

That higher part of your brain that I discussed in Part One is your best friend when it comes to time management. In reality, time management is quite simple:

1. Write out your to-do list, calendar everything, and then throw away your to-do list.
2. Do only what's on your calendar.
3. Feel the feelings that come up and process them; allow urges to do other things without giving in to those urges.

I just want to point out that I said it was simple, not easy. You've had years of believing that time is an issue and your brain has been looking for proof that that's true—but that's a lie.

In Part One of this book, I described the Motivational Triad in which your lower brain is motivated to seek pleasure, avoid pain, and expend as little energy as possible. This is incredibly important to understand when it comes to time management because learning a new way of thinking, feeling, and acting takes energy, so don't be surprised when that Toddler part of your brain throws a temper tantrum when you want to start being a Smarter Accountant with your time.

Just know that I've got you. Retraining your brain is not only possible —it's life-changing.

Becoming a Smarter Accountant means not only knowing how to plan with your higher brain and how to make decisions ahead of time but also how to make sure that you follow through on your plan. With practice, you will learn to not give in to your lower brain's temper tantrums and distractions: you will plan your time (being kind to that future version of *you* that has to follow the plan), you will know exactly what you're going to do and when, and you will get it done no matter what.

CHAPTER FIVE: IF I'M SO SMART, WHY AM I NOT AS PRODUCTIVE AS I'D LIKE TO BE?

Jeff's Story

Jeff was a partner in a small firm and had worked his way up from entry-level associate to partner over 25 years with the same firm. He had a long history in the accounting profession, starting in the days of 10-column paper to manage financials to now using the latest technology available to help accountants be more productive and efficient.

Jeff was not only willing to learn everything he could about using technology: he was also a fast learner, and he enjoyed trying different apps and programs to see what would work best for him and the firm at large. He was fine with the workflow system that had been implemented and could see its merits.

The issue Jeff was having was with his productivity. He just wasn't being as productive and efficient as he would like to be.

It didn't matter whether he used a paper planner or a computer program like Outlook: he just couldn't seem to produce the amount of work he wanted, or needed, to maintain the billable hours he was contractually obligated to complete.

Although he worked an average of 60 hours a week, he wasn't happy with what he had to show for his time. He always seemed to be busy but that didn't mean he was producing anything of value.

Even when he was at home with his wife and children, he noticed that he rarely sat down to relax but that he still wasn't as productive as he'd like to be. He would often get to the office on Monday morning and, when asked what he did that weekend, he was at a loss.

If you asked the other people in his life at work and home, they wouldn't describe Jeff as "lazy" but, deep down, he just didn't like his busyness for the sake of being busy. He wanted to get a better handle on his productivity and to feel better about his contributions both at work and at home.

Many times, as he sat in the office at the end of the workday, he asked himself, "If I'm so smart, why am I not as productive as I'd like to be?"

The Truth About Productivity

The issue that I see for most accountants is thinking that a to-do list is the answer to their productivity issues. But here's the problem with to-do lists—they *don't* make you more productive because of how your brain interprets a list of things to do.

The truth is that, when you're solely working off a to-do list, things don't get done efficiently, other things get in the way, you feel confused and scattered, and you wonder why you feel like you can never get ahead. Your lower, Toddler brain sees a long list of things to do and cannot delineate between something being simple versus complicated—it sees everything as urgent and overwhelming.

To your lower brain, all items on a to-do list look the same because this part of the brain cannot do one very important thing—put things into context. It cannot make intelligent decisions about the individual items on your to-do list, and instead dramatically sees them all as one big problem that cannot be solved.

To become more productive, you have to create space in your brain to process things more efficiently and effectively. You do need to get everything out of your brain and onto paper but, once you've calendared everything (and I mean everything!), you need to throw that to-do list away.

The issue is that most accountants will write down everything they have to do and then become completely overwhelmed. Do you know what doesn't help you to be productive? The feeling of overwhelm!

To be more productive, you have to become a Smarter Accountant. You have to understand what's happening in your brain when you have things you'd like or need to get done. Otherwise, you'll just take action and stay busy without getting the results you want.

The biggest mistake that most people make when trying to be productive is focusing on the actions that they're going to take and calendaring those actions. It's how most accountants believe they can manage their productivity, but then they wind up with the same issues that Jeff experienced at the beginning of this chapter.

For example, they'll put "Call XYZ client", "Review the ABC file", or "Make an appointment with the doctor" on their calendar. Sounds okay, right? Wrong!

If you want to be more productive, you need to schedule results, not actions. Why? Because when you calendar your time to produce something, you need to have a result when you're done, not just time spent.

You need to give yourself a time limit to get the result and you need to honor that time limit no matter what. This might be challenging for perfectionistic accountants to hear (yes, I'm talking to you), but you have to be willing to not do A+ work. Gasp!

Perfectionism is the arch-enemy of productivity. If you have more time later to edit something, that's fine but, to be productive, you need to follow the "Done is better than perfect" adage.

For greater productivity, you have to have a plan for the result you want to produce, give yourself a time limit, don't try to be perfect on the first go-around, and—the most important thing—clean up your thinking, at least at the beginning of each day, but often throughout the day as well.

A Smarter Accountant knows the power of the Model in managing their brain and being able to produce at a very high level. They know how to be productive, and efficient, and how not to feel overwhelmed in the process.

Unchecking the Box

So how is it possible to be more productive? The Model is the answer because managing your mind is the key that you've been missing.

To be a Smarter Accountant, you need to understand the difference between productivity and taking action. Most accountants are busy (actually very busy) but are not getting more done in less time because they're not using their prefrontal cortex to manage what they do.

As I have shared, productivity comes from what you produce, not from how busy you are. In order to be more productive, you have to be clear as to what you are producing and how long you are giving yourself to produce it.

I can honestly tell you that this has been a huge game changer for me, especially at work. I'm able to typically get more done than anyone else in the office, even when I work less hours.

How is that possible? Because being a Smarter Accountant means not being busy for the sake of keeping busy—it's about producing result after result, deciding in advance how long I'm going to give myself to achieve the result, not getting distracted from the task at hand, sticking with the plan no matter what, and managing my mind the entire time.

When you use feelings like efficient, focused, and clear, the actions fueled by those feelings are going to produce at a much higher rate than feeling overwhelmed, frustrated, or confused. Just like you would choose the best gasoline to put into an expensive, luxury vehicle, you need to fuel your productivity with the best fuel possible.

By getting clear about what has to get done, deciding how much time to give yourself to get the result, and then scheduling the result on your calendar, you have set yourself up for greater productivity.

When it comes to productivity, it doesn't matter how many hours you've worked, how busy you are, or how stressed you are. The only thing that matters is the results that you have produced.

Thankfully, as a Smarter Accountant, you can become much more productive because you will understand that managing your mind has to come first. The only reason you haven't been as productive as you'd like to be is because of your unmanaged brain.

Here's what a typical Model looks like for an unmanaged accountant:

Circumstance: Tax project due by 6/1

Thought: I'm getting nowhere with this project

Feeling: Frustrated

Actions: I tell myself that I have no idea where to start; I tell myself I'm not being productive; I tell myself I get burned-out of it easily because I think too much about the project; I don't break down the project into smaller results; I procrastinate; I compare myself to others in the office; I question what I should be doing

Result: I don't get anywhere with the project

The key here is that it wasn't the tax project due by 6/1 that was the problem—it was the thought "I'm getting nowhere with this project" that created the feeling of frustration. The question I ask all my coaching clients at some point is, "Why would you choose to think that unhelpful thought?" It might seem true to you, but you have to question whether it's useful or not; whether it's helping you to get the result you want and helping you to be as productive as you want.

Here's what a Model looks like for a Smarter Accountant:

Circumstance: Tax project due by 6/1

Thought: I am getting somewhere with this project

Feeling: Focused

Actions: I start by breaking down the project; I tell myself I've got this; I tell myself I'm being productive; I get clear about the results I want and the time I want to give myself; I calendar results, not action; I follow my calendar no matter what; I don't procrastinate; I don't compare myself to others in the office; I stay focused on the results I want

Result: I get somewhere with the project

The beauty of being a Smarter Accountant is that you'll begin to notice the unhelpful feelings that come up. You'll begin to understand your unique brain better and even anticipate what it could come up with that might derail the results you want.

When I work with my coaching clients on better productivity in the Smarter Accountant Program, they begin to become aware of the sneaky way their lower brain tries to distract them from doing work. They're amazed at how strong-willed the lower brain is because, just like a Toddler, it wants what it wants when it wants it, and most of the time it does not want to do things that involve effort.

But, thankfully, my clients learn how to catch their brain, they become aware of the signs of a temper tantrum, and they learn how to create a plan of action for those times. By learning when and how to direct their brain, they're able to blow their minds with how much more productive they can be.

Summary

As my coaching clients learn how to become Smarter Accountants, they also learn to approach their brain as a scientist would, trying to understand the inner workings of the subject of their experiment—them! It helps to detach themselves from being the person experiencing their brain, to instead being the observer of their brain.

At first, it can be a little jarring and sometimes even embarrassing to have the awareness of how childlike our brains can be, but with knowledge comes power. A Smarter Accountant understands their brain's patterns, its limiting beliefs, and the effects of their thoughts, feelings, and actions.

The fact that you're even reading this book is an important first step. Once you read this material, you're not going to be able to help but notice a negative emotion and then realize that it's not coming from a circumstance—it can only come from a thought about a circumstance.

That's when things can change dramatically. Another tool I teach my Smarter Accountant coaching clients is understanding the difference between emotional childhood and emotional adulthood:

Emotional childhood is when you blame people, places, and things for how you feel. You blame circumstances for how you feel, giving your power away in the process.

Emotional adulthood is when you take 100% responsibility for how you feel. You acknowledge that it's only your thoughts that can create your feelings, not circumstances. You take your power back to create whatever you want for your life.

Being a Smarter Accountant means spending more time in emotional adulthood than in emotional childhood. Because of this, you become much more productive because you understand why you feel the way you do and you also know how to deliberately feel any constructive emotion.

CHAPTER SIX: IF I'M SO SMART, WHY DO I GET STUCK COMPARING MYSELF TO OTHERS?

Kendra's Story

Kendra decided to study accounting a little later than most. After high school, she decided to join the military and, once she finished serving her time, she chose to go back to school for an accounting degree.

Not only was she older than most of the students in her class, she was also balancing school, a part-time job, being a wife, and being a mom to her young daughter. Although she had a lot on her plate, she completed her undergraduate accounting degree, was finishing up her Master's, was planning on taking the CPA exam, and was at the point where she was going to be interviewing for an accounting position.

The issue that Kendra was dealing with was a lack of confidence and caring too much about what others thought of her. This latter concern was holding her back from putting herself out there.

Whether it was simply believing that what she had to share in a conversation was valuable, or having the confidence to apply for positions that she was qualified for, she had a hard time not comparing herself to others and then feeling despair.

Her dream was to have the confidence to not care what other people think, not compare herself to others, and be able to own her unique gifts and talents. She was intelligent, loved learning, was articulate, and wanted to eventually help a company grow as their controller, but it was as if there was a wall of self-doubt that kept being put in her path.

She was so used to being in the background, not taking charge, and letting others make decisions for her that she believed she wasn't as capable as the other students she went to school with. She constantly compared herself to others and always came up short in her mind.

She knew she was smart, having one of the highest GPAs in her graduating class, but she just didn't have the level of self-confidence that she would like. She tried ignoring her feelings of self-doubt but then someone would do or say something and she'd fall right back into her pattern of compare and despair.

Many times she looked around at other women, mothers, and accountants and asked herself, "If I'm so smart, why do I get stuck comparing myself to others?"

The Truth About Comparing and Despairing

The issue that I see for most accountants when it comes to comparing themselves to others is that it affects so many areas of their lives, not just their work. It can affect their relationships, self-confidence, ability to set and achieve goals, and much more.

If you're not familiar with the term "compare and despair", it refers to our tendency to distress ourselves by comparing ourselves and our situations with someone else's. It's a vicious cycle of making a comparison that puts us in a negative light, and then feeling horrible and less capable because of the comparison.

But before you beat yourself up for your tendency to compare yourself to others, let me help you out—it's completely natural. Your brain has been hardwired to compare you to others and it starts putting this into action at a relatively young age.

In order to survive, the human brain has a tribe mentality and looks for ways to understand your relationship with the rest of the tribe and how you fit in. Your lower brain equates rejection with death. Therefore, not being accepted or valuable is quite threatening.

As you learned about the survival of the fittest in school, your brain's motivation for survival has been to measure you against others, build connections that keep you safe, and be on the lookout for any threats. You're not just looking for differences in people and situations, you are also hardwired to see if those differences are better or worse.

When it comes to our tendency to compare and despair, there have been some interesting studies done to understand how this inclination affects our happiness and contentment. There have even been some interesting studies of Olympic medal winners to compare the happiness level of each winner.

At first glance, you would think that the Gold winner would be the happiest, the Silver winner the second happiest, and the Bronze winner would be the least happy. But that's not what these studies discovered.

Because of the tendency to compare and despair, the Silver winner was looking at the one person, the Gold winner, to compare themselves to and thinking "I was so close!", thereby creating the feeling of unworthiness. However, the Bronze winner was looking at *all* the people they needed to beat to be on the podium, thinking, "This is amazing!" and feeling happier than the Silver winner.

The truth is that your brain is constantly looking to see who you may be in competition with and determining who is "winning". This means that you believe you need to accumulate validation and gold stars in order to feel good about yourself.

When you add your brain's natural tendency to compare, as well as being taught at an early age that competition is good, it's no wonder you compare and despair. You're constantly scanning to see if you measure up and looking for those measurements to determine if you should feel better or worse about yourself.

When the cycle of compare and despair becomes a habit, you are not only measuring your self-worth against others, you can also begin doubting decisions or getting stuck in confusion. If you have a habit of looking to the past, comparing it to the present, and then feeling bad about a decision, you are also strengthening the compare and despair cycle.

When you haven't worked on understanding and managing your brain, you will mistakenly believe you need to be different, or have a different situation, in order to feel happy, but that's not true. The only way to get out of the cycle of compare and despair and feel better is to change the way you are thinking.

A Smarter Accountant understands how important the Model is to getting unstuck from the trap of comparing themselves to others. They know what's happening, why it's happening, and how to stop the compare and despair cycle.

Unchecking the Box

So, if it's so natural, how do you stop it? The Model is the answer because managing your mind is the key to not getting, and staying, stuck.

To be a Smarter Accountant, you need to understand the difference between a circumstance and a thought. In other words, you need to know the difference between the facts of someone else's life versus yours and your optional thoughts about those facts.

For most of us, our brain's natural tendency to compare for survival can come in the form of thoughts like:

- I'm not smart enough to get that job.
- My marriage will never be as good as hers.
- He got the promotion because he can work later than I can.
- It must be nice to be able to drive a car like that.
- I could never pull off a hairstyle like that.
- I'm trying to eat healthy and she gets to drink soda and look like that?
- Why does he get the better office?

It's important to first uncover those repetitive thoughts, especially if you've been thinking negatively about yourself or your situation for some time. Those are the thoughts creating feelings like self-doubt and regret.

Interestingly, when you have issues with comparing yourself to others, you most likely also have issues with "imposter syndrome".

This is when you feel that you'll be uncovered as a fraud for being unworthy of what you've worked so hard to achieve.

With imposter syndrome, you typically experience that insidious sense that you're out of your league, not good enough, that you are only in your position because you got lucky, or that sooner or later you will be found out. It's usually a heaviness you carry around, just waiting for someone to "discover" you're not who you pretend to be.

Remember what I explained in Part One—because your thoughts are always fueling your emotions, if you've been dealing with comparing yourself to others or suffering from imposter syndrome, it's no wonder you haven't been feeling great. In addition, what you think about yourself and your decisions will not only affect how you feel but also determine the actions you take.

To be a Smarter Accountant, you need to have the awareness of the thoughts creating your compare and despair cycle and own them, not just sweep them under the rug. When learning how to manage your brain, it can be tempting to notice that you feel bad and want to jump right away to feel better without getting clear about what created the bad feeling in the first place. But it's much more useful to understand the cause.

A Smarter Accountant doesn't bury their head in the sand. They understand what's within their power and they use that power to create the results they want.

If the comparison leads you to feel worse about yourself, you have to question its usefulness. When you feel self-doubt, jealousy, or resentment, those feelings will never fuel useful action.

By getting clear about the thoughts causing feelings like those, you can choose more helpful, productive, and effective thoughts. The truth is that, when you understand the cause, you have the power to change the effect.

Thankfully, as a Smarter Accountant, you can override the tendency to struggle with comparison because you will understand that managing your mind has to come first. The only reason you have been comparing and despairing is because of your unmanaged brain.

Here's what a typical Model looks like for an unmanaged accountant:

Circumstance: Connection on LinkedIn posted a promotion

Thought: I'm not as far along as others with the same work experience

Feeling: Self-doubt

Actions: I tell myself that I'm not as good as others; I tell myself I haven't done enough; I don't look at what I have accomplished; I beat myself up for what I don't know; I resent others' accomplishments; I look for ways that I'm an imposter; I compare myself to others; I don't look for ways I can grow; I don't set goals; I question my choices; I question whether I know what I'm doing

Result: I prevent myself from going further

The key here is that the post on LinkedIn about the person's promotion wasn't the problem—it was the thought, "I'm not as far along as others with the same work experience", that created the feeling of self-doubt. Although most of us experience feelings of self-doubt, it's our actions, inactions, and reactions that become an issue because they result in our not being, doing, or having what we want.

Here's what a Model looks like for a Smarter Accountant:

Circumstance: Connection on LinkedIn posted a promotion

Thought: If it's possible for them, it's possible for me

Feeling: Hopeful

Actions: I look at what I've accomplished so far; I reach out to the LinkedIn connection and congratulate them; I explore the direction that I'd like to go with my career; I look for others who have done what I'd like to do; I use their success as inspiration; I narrow down what I'd like to focus on over the next 30 days; I create a plan for the steps I need to take; I explore more possibilities; I reach out to other connections; I get clear on what I want

Result: I allow for possibilities

Being a Smarter Accountant doesn't stop your lower brain from comparing—it just allows you to recognize what's happening and to be able to pivot. There are plenty of times when I see what someone else is doing or what they've accomplished and I fall into the comparison trap (thanks to social media!), but I just don't choose to stay in the compare and despair cycle for too long.

When I coach clients in the Smarter Accountant Program, I make sure that they don't beat themselves up for having a human brain but, instead, create a much greater awareness of what is happening and why. As I will continue to share throughout this book, the beauty of knowing the cause is that you then have the power to change the effect.

Summary

It's important to understand that comparing yourself to others makes it incredibly difficult, if not impossible, to value your own efforts and progress. Despite what you might have been told, comparison is not as motivating as you might think.

As my coaching clients learn how to become Smarter Accountants, they open their minds to so many more possibilities. They learn how to shine a light on their unhelpful thoughts and choose instead to direct their brain more intentionally.

They come to understand that, if the feeling of self-doubt is caused by their thoughts, then the feeling of self-confidence can be as well. For accountants, this can be a big wake-up call—your level of knowledge, the school you graduated from, the experience you do or don't have, and the number of letters after your last name are just neutral circumstances—they don't mean anything until you make them mean something.

So, if comparison has been a big issue for you, the concept of "cognitive dissonance" is important. This is the scientific term for the discomfort that results from holding two conflicting beliefs, and it's what happens in your brain when you're stuck between an unhelpful thought and a helpful thought.

Thankfully, there is a way to deal with cognitive dissonance and it's called "Bridge Thoughts." If you've ever seen one of those rope bridges that have wooden planks tied together, that cross from one side of a riverbank to another, that's the image I learned when it comes to Bridge Thoughts.

Bridge Thoughts are a series of thoughts that can get you from one side of the river to the other. They are the planks on the bridge, helping you to gradually lessen your brain's grip on an unintentional thought and moving you towards an intentional thought—in other words, from one that's unhelpful to one that is helpful.

An example of a Bridge Thought between "I hate my job" and "I love my job" would be "I have a job". As you can see, "I have a job" feels better than "I hate my job" and, more importantly, it's believable.

Remember, you have to work on choosing thoughts that are believable or your brain won't let them "stick". With Bridge Thoughts, you're simply giving your brain other optional, believable thoughts that can gradually take you to the thought you'd like to believe.

Hopefully, you can see that being a Smarter Accountant means having various tools in your toolbelt and, again, understanding the instruction manual for your brain—the Model. By getting a better sense of control over your brain's natural inclination to compare you to others, you'll open up so many more possibilities for yourself.

CHAPTER SEVEN: IF I'M SO SMART, WHY DO I HAVE SUCH DIFFICULTY WITH CRITICISM?

Mark's Story

Mark was a financial analyst at a large healthcare organization, trying to work his way up the corporate ladder. Although the organization as a whole was dealing with the detrimental effects of the pandemic on its patients and employees, they were doing the best they could to manage employees working both in-person and remotely.

The finance department was one of the groups that were continuing to work remotely, making some employees happy and others frustrated. Mark was doing what he could to be a team player, trying to manage the expectations of his boss while supporting his colleagues, but he found it challenging to be recognized for his hard work while working remotely.

Even with the new hybrid situation, the department heads were performing mid-year reviews and it was now time for Mark's review. He told his girlfriend that he knew that reviews were a necessary part of the job, but he couldn't help feeling horrible afterwards.

Ever since Mark was younger, he had had a hard time receiving criticism, often being upset for weeks due to a remark a teacher made on his report card or something a sports coach said to him. He struggled with moving past other people's feedback and critiques, often feeling a good deal of shame.

He knew he was intelligent and a hard worker, but he dreaded hearing criticism, especially from his employer. Sometimes, he became so worried about negative feedback that he became a people pleaser, trying to control other people's opinions of him.

After he received this year's mid-year review, all he could focus on was the one or two "needs improvement" ratings and not on all the "meeting or exceeding expectations" ones. He felt inadequate after his review and spent a lot of time trying to figure out what he had done wrong.

He could see how much it was distracting him and how it was affecting how he showed up around his boss, but he couldn't stop. A trusted colleague tried to help him deal with the mid-year review feedback, but he wasn't getting through to Mark.

At the end of each workday, and even when he wasn't at work, Mark would say to himself, "If I'm so smart, why do I have such difficulty with criticism?"

The Truth About Criticism

In this day and age of social media, product reviews, and Yelp, you are probably asked many times for feedback and reviews. You may also use other people's feedback and reviews before you hire someone or purchase something.

For example, before I go anywhere on vacation, I always check Trip Advisor and read the reviews and comments about the places and activities I'm planning on visiting. I also scour the reviews of a book

I'm interested in reading to get a feel for whether the book is worth my time, and I will check the reviews on OpenTable before I try a new restaurant.

So if we live at a time when reviews and feedback are so common, then why aren't we better at giving and receiving feedback and criticism? To answer that, let's distinguish between the two by first looking at the dictionary definitions:

Criticize (dictionary)—to find fault; judge unfavorably or harshly; to make judgments as to merits and faults

Feedback (dictionary)—a reaction or response to a particular process or activity

The important thing to notice is that the dictionary definition of feedback isn't about a person, it's about the actions or process the person was involved in. Although both involve an evaluation, criticism uses the words "judge" and "fault", making it seem much more personal to the giver or receiver.

Now that we are clear on the dictionary definitions, I want to give you a different perspective that a fellow life coach shared:

Criticize (new perspective)—the action one takes which is caused by negative emotions; action taken with the intention to release negative emotions in order to feel better

Feedback (new perspective)—the action one takes in order to help or convey information; action taken from a neutral place with the intention of informing

As you learned in Part One, the Model shows you why you and others take certain actions—because of a feeling. Remember, feelings are the only things that causes actions.

As you can see with the new perspective of the difference between criticism and feedback, it all comes down to intention and how you or others were feeling before taking action. Whether you are on the receiving or giving end, determining whether it's criticism or feedback will always be based on the intention behind it, and the good news is that it's up to you to decide.

In essence, the words someone says about you are neutral and you get to decide whether you want to think that they are feedback or criticism. You get to decide whether the person was feeling negative or neutral, even if you can't be sure.

Just knowing this delineation is the first important step to learning the subtle art of receiving criticism. It could mean the difference between a powerful opportunity for growth and a frustrating game of shame.

A Smarter Accountant has the awareness of what their lower, Toddler brain is making someone's words mean, and they decide on purpose how they want to think about it to be in control of how they feel, what they do or don't do, and their results. They use the Model to determine the best way to interpret someone's words, making it much easier to handle criticism.

Unchecking the Box

While we believe we would love to go through life without having to deal with criticism, this is partly because of what our brain makes criticism mean about our safety. The interesting thing is that our primitive brain sees criticism as dangerous to our survival because, if we aren't accepted by the tribe, or if we are found to be lacking in some way, we could be ostracized and die.

It may sound overly dramatic but that's what the primitive part of your brain thinks. It's always on the lookout for things it considers dangerous, and criticism is threatening to this part of your brain.

It also has a negativity bias, often interpreting other people's words in a negative light without your awareness that it's happening. We have a knee-jerk response to someone's words and don't question whether our interpretation is true or not, oftentimes because it feels true.

When it comes to dealing with criticism, to be a Smarter Accountant you need to understand the difference between a circumstance and a thought. In other words, you need to know the difference between the facts of someone's words and your optional thoughts about those facts.

Once again, the Model will show you why this is important because, although we don't have control over most circumstances, we always have the power over our thoughts about circumstances. Everything below the circumstance line of the Model is within your control.

The tricky thing is that, when it comes to deciphering between a circumstance (fact) or a thought (opinion), and between feedback or criticism, your brain will involuntarily be swayed by what's already familiar, even in the face of evidence to the contrary. It's the reason why there are still people in the world today who will argue that the Earth is flat.

For example, if you already believe that you aren't good at your job, when you receive something like your yearly review, you may interpret comments as negative and as criticism about you and your capabilities. Your brain will automatically filter this new information and confirm it against old beliefs, whether those beliefs are helpful or not.

Thankfully, as a Smarter Accountant, you can understand the subtle art of both giving and receiving criticism because you will understand that managing your mind has to come first. The only reason you have difficulty with criticism is because of your unmanaged brain.

Here's what a typical Model looks like for an unmanaged accountant:

Circumstance: Boss wrote in yearly review "Needs to spend more time reviewing work before handing off to manager"

Thought: I can never seem to do things right

Feeling: Inadequate

Actions: Let the review negatively affect me; wish the boss would see me differently; spin in confusion about what to do; complain about the review; complain about the boss; tell myself I might not be cut out for the job; worry about the future; procrastinate; look for more ways to criticize myself; don't see where the boss's words could be feedback instead of criticism; don't allow myself to be pleased with all the other areas where I got a good rating

Result: I am more likely to do things wrong

The key here is that it wasn't what was written in the review that was the problem—it was the thought, "I can never seem to do things right", that created the feeling of inadequacy. That feeling is never going to drive the action necessary to move forward and do what needs to be done, or to see the boss's words as feedback rather than criticism.

Here's what a Model looks like for a Smarter Accountant:

Circumstance: Boss wrote in yearly review "Needs to spend more time reviewing work before handing off to manager"

Thought: This is valuable feedback

Feeling: Open

Actions: See the boss positively; see the feedback positively; see myself positively; take an honest look at where I do need to spend more time reviewing work before handing it off to a manager; follow up with the boss and ask for his suggestions regarding how to improve in this area; create a plan for allocating more time on reviewing work; see where the boss's words were feedback instead of criticism; allow myself to be pleased with all the other areas where I got a good rating

Result: I add even more value to myself and my job

The Smarter Accountant may have noticed a twinge of inadequacy with the boss's comment, but then chose to feel open, on purpose. By choosing the thought, "This is valuable feedback", they created the feeling of openness and their actions created the result that proved their thought—they added even more value to themselves and their job.

The coaching clients in the Smarter Accountant Program understand that, while they cannot stop people from having opinions or offering feedback, they do have the power to decide on purpose what they want to think about it. By becoming Smarter Accountants, they understand that they always have a choice.

Summary

Please understand that I'm not saying feedback or criticism doesn't sting, but what I am saying is that it doesn't have to linger. The best gift you give yourself when you learn how to manage your mind is taking your power back.

As I mentioned before, another helpful way to handle criticism is to become aware of whether you are believing something is a circumstance (fact) or a thought (opinion). Here is the difference:

If it's a circumstance (fact), everyone would agree and it would NOT create a negative or positive feeling.

If it's a thought (opinion), others could agree or disagree and it usually creates either a negative or positive feeling.

Here's an example to help explain:

Circumstance (fact)—"Your billable hours were lower this year by 100 hours"

Thought (opinion)—"You aren't as productive as everyone else in your department"

However, you choose to interpret someone's words—whether in writing or verbally—you get to decide how you want to categorize them. Is it criticism, feedback, a circumstance, or a thought? It's helpful to do this both before (if possible) and after someone shares an evaluation or comment with you.

If you have time beforehand, then I suggest you decide on purpose how you want to feel before you go into the situation. If you decide you want to be calm and open-minded, then you could choose thoughts like "A yearly review is not a reflection of my worth as a CPA" or "I always try to do my best no matter what".

If you already have your review or know what someone has said, it's important that afterwards you also ask yourself whether this is feedback or criticism. Even though the distinction between the two is the intention of the other person and you never really know for sure what their intention is, you usually have a pretty good idea. Here is the difference:

Was the person trying to pass along some information that they believe is helpful? Then it was probably feedback.

Were they feeling negative emotions and trying to make themselves feel better? Then it was probably criticism.

For example:

Feedback (from your mother-in-law)—"When my children were picky eaters, I found it helpful to have them in the kitchen helping me make the food so they were part of the process."

Criticism—"It's very frustrating to watch your children because they are the pickiest eaters I've ever seen; you really need to get that under control better."

Knowing that a person may be complaining because they are frustrated and trying to make themselves feel better can help to diffuse the situation. It can also be helpful to notice when exaggerations or over-generalizations are made because any negativity on the part of the giver is about them, not you.

If you tend to assume the worst in someone, then it can also be beneficial to have someone outside the situation who can help you understand whether you are getting feedback or criticism. Remember, your brain is biased towards what you already believe about yourself and others.

The expression, "Take what you like and leave the rest", can be helpful when you tend to be too hard on yourself, but it's also important to not miss the opportunity that feedback, and sometimes even criticism, may provide. It may be worth finding a "nugget" of truth if it could be beneficial personally or professionally, as long as it moves you forward instead of keeping you stuck or making you feel worse.

You can apply this to any area of your life, whether your mother-in-law likes to compare how she raised her children, you are dreading the upcoming parent–teacher conference, or someone flips you off on the highway. It's all so much easier when you learn to distinguish between a circumstance (fact) or a thought (opinion) and between feedback or criticism.

A Smarter Accountant may not like criticism but they understand how to deal with it better than most. They know how to manage their brain, and how to move forward in a way that is helpful to them and their career.

CHAPTER EIGHT: IF I'M SO SMART, WHY AM I NOT MAKING THE MONEY I WANT?

Danielle's Story

Danielle was a CPA, a wife, and a mother of two teenage daughters. She had a good job in a medium-sized public accounting firm and had received the standard pay raises each year.

Although Danielle's husband was also a hard worker, they never seemed to be able to make ends meet. Even from the beginning of their marriage, money was a struggle for them, often causing arguments and creating problems in their relationship.

The truth was that Danielle grew up in a low- to middle-class neighborhood and watched her parents struggle to make ends meet as well. Her parents also often fought about money issues, which she and her younger brother witnessed.

Part of the reason Danielle chose an accounting career was that she wanted to have a better understanding of finances and not repeat the same mistakes her parents had made. She wanted to not only understand how to account for other people's money, but also to earn a good living doing it.

The latest issue was that she and her husband had accumulated $50,000 in credit card debt, in addition to their mortgage and car loans. It seemed like they would never get out from under the pile of debt or be able to help their children pay for college.

On top of being frustrated by their debt, Danielle was also embarrassed by it. She felt a lot of shame from the fact that she was a CPA with a good job, yet she just couldn't get a handle on her money.

Because both she and her husband were frustrated and embarrassed, they often looked at ways to drastically cut their expenses rather than how each of them could make more money. They were so focused on the money they spent, and feeling bad about it, that they just couldn't change their scarcity mindset around money.

At the end of each month when Danielle would balance her checkbook, she would often say to herself, "If I'm so smart, why am I not making the money I want?"

The Truth About Money

As an accountant, you most likely believe you know how to handle other people's money and finances. But let me ask you a few questions:

- How do you *feel* about money?
- What is your relationship with *your* money?
- Do you know *how to* money (yes as a verb)?

Most of us, myself included, have a "money belief lineage"—a set of beliefs about money that we're taught from an early age. Those beliefs are often passed down from generation to generation with tweaks and adjustments along the way.

For example, your great-grandmother may have stayed home to raise children and had the belief that there's never enough money—one that she passed on to her children; your grandfather may have had beliefs that he inherited from his parents about how money "doesn't grow on trees"; your mother and father probably inherited their parents' beliefs about what it takes to make a decent living, and passed those beliefs on to you.

We've all been taught various things about money, from various people, which have culminated in our own set of beliefs about money. Some of them might be helpful but, if you checked the box in the Introduction, "You're not making the money you want to make", you probably have some unhelpful beliefs about money.

I also want to point out that, if you are a parent, it's important to address your money beliefs so that you don't continue an unhelpful "money belief lineage" with them as well. If money beliefs have been passed down to you, there's a very good chance that you are also passing those beliefs on to your children.

The first thing you need to know when it comes to the truth about money is that, as you have relationships with the people, places, and things in your life, you also have a relationship with money. The reason it's important to see money in this way, as something you have a relationship with, is that the Model will be able to help you make the money you want.

The key is understanding that a relationship with anything or anyone is based on your thoughts about the thing or the person, and the Model is a powerful tool to improve your relationship with money. It teaches you that, although circumstances are often not within your control, your thoughts, feelings, actions, and, ultimately, your results, are all within your control.

So what does that have to do with making the money you want? Everything! The reason why making more money can seem so difficult and daunting is that there are so many people's opinions about what you should be doing—invest here, move there, sell this, buy that—it's no wonder you can't figure out what to do.

I'm here to make it super simple for you—focus on your brain.

When it comes to money, you need to understand what you are thinking when you are making money, and also what you are thinking when you aren't. The Model shows you that your thoughts and beliefs about money are going to fuel the action you take (or don't take), which will ultimately create your money results.

As a Smarter Accountant, you understand that the money you currently have is simply a result that your brain produced by virtue of your thoughts, feelings, and actions. So, if you want to change the result, you have to first get clear on the thoughts and beliefs that created the current result, and then choose more empowering thoughts and beliefs that will create the result you want.

For example, if you currently make $100,000 a year but would like to make $200,000, your current beliefs that created the $100,000 are *not* the beliefs that will create $200,000. You must become aware of what you are currently thinking and believing about money, improve your relationship with money (i.e. your thoughts about money), and use the higher, prefrontal cortex part of your brain to manage your lower brain's tendency to think $100,000-producing thoughts.

In addition, accountants also tend to have a "time plus effort" perception when it comes to making money, leading most to have huge issues with time management and burnout. What I encourage you to do is shift your beliefs about needing more time and effort to make more money, and instead switch to a belief that value is what creates more money.

The truth is that you do not need to spend more time working or put in more effort to make more money. That is just a belief that you've probably never considered challenging before.

Instead, consider this—what if the more value you provide, whether it's to your boss, your company, or your clients, and the more willing you are to receive money—the more money you'll make? What if, instead of equating time with money, you instead equate value with more money? What would be possible then?

Unchecking the Box

While the whole world has been challenged by the recent pandemic in one way or another, one of the most challenging financial issues is what's referred to as "money insecurity"—a belief that you don't have enough or that you aren't good enough to have more. The reason this is so common during challenging times, like the ones we've been facing, is that everything that was a concern in the past will often be triggered and come to the forefront of our minds.

Unfortunately, if you were worried before, especially around the subject of money, you are going to look for all the reasons to be worried now. Again, this is both a blessing and a curse of having a human brain.

The truth is that your brain is a pattern-seeking machine and will always look to prove what you believe to be true. If you believe in lack and scarcity, your brain will filter out anything that supports the opposite—abundance.

To explain how your brain's filter works, here's an analogy that I've often used with my coaching clients in the Smarter Accountant Program. Imagine you were in the market to buy a red car and all of a sudden all you see are red cars on the road. The reason this happens is that your brain has a filtering system that shows you what's important to you. It's called the "Reticular Activating System" and is pretty amazing.

The issue though is that, if your default way of thinking creates worry and insecurity, that's exactly what your brain's Reticular Activating System will show you more of. Just like the red cars, your brain will offer you more thoughts that create the feeling of worry and insecurity.

Until you change the default setting on your brain, it will continue to show you more and more proof of what you believe, whether it's helpful or not. Until you change the cause, you cannot change the effect.

Although the impetus for your concerns about money may have begun many years ago, possibly from your childhood, or from when you became an adult earning your own money, thankfully it doesn't have to continue to be an issue any longer. A Smarter Accountant knows how to change the default patterns in their brain and create much better results in the process.

When using the Model, money can be a circumstance but it can also be a result. Either way, the Model will show you why you have the money you currently have as well as how to have the money you want.

If money is in the circumstance line of the Model, you have control over what you choose to think about it. If money is in the result line of the Model, you have control over the actions you take, the feeling that fuels those actions, and the thought that creates that feeling.

In other words, money can either be a fact or a result. It can be a fact that you can always improve by what you think, feel, and do, or it can be a result that you can reverse engineer by using the Model backward (more on this in the Summary of this chapter).

As a Smarter Accountant, you get to not only choose your relationship with money as well as how much money you want to have, but you also get to decide on the value you're going to offer in exchange for money. The best part about being a Smarter Accountant is that money isn't an issue when you have a managed brain.

Here's what a typical Model looks like for an unmanaged accountant:

Circumstance: My salary is $50,000 a year

Thought: I don't make enough money

Feeling: Scarcity

Actions: Beat myself up for not making more money; complain about not making enough money; tell myself I'm not capable of making more; worry about the future; don't look for ways to make more; don't speak to boss about how I can add more value to make more money; don't look at other options; don't appreciate the money I do make

Result: I prevent myself from making more money

The key here is that it wasn't the salary or the amount of money that was the problem—it was the thought, "I don't make enough money", that created the feeling of scarcity. The feeling of scarcity is never going to drive the actions necessary to make more money, find ways to create more value or explore other options.

Here's what a Model looks like for a Smarter Accountant:

Circumstance: My salary is $50,000 a year

Thought: I have what it takes to make more money

Feeling: Motivated

Actions: Don't beat myself up for the amount of money I make; tell myself I'm totally capable of making more; set a goal for how much money I want to make and by when; look for ways to make more; speak to boss about how I can add more value to make more money; look at other options; look at classes I can take to uplevel my expertise; appreciate the money I do make while also wanting more; research accounting positions in other industries; reach out to people in those industries; find out what else I need to start doing to make more money

Result: I do what it takes to make more money

The Smarter Accountant may have not been thrilled with the $50,000 a year salary, but they also know that a feeling of scarcity will never give them the result they want. They also know that they can choose how they want to think about their current salary, in a way that is helpful, but they can also put the amount of money they do want to make in the result line of the Model and work backwards.

One of the many benefits of becoming a Smarter Accountant is that you have so much more control over money than you previously thought you had. Whether you're an employee or an entrepreneur, you can make the money you want when you learn the power of managing your brain.

Summary

Hopefully, you can see that you have so much more power when it comes to making money than you probably realize. If money simply comes from an exchange of value, just consider all the options that might be available to you!

It's important to understand that the more helpful your thoughts are about your current circumstance of money, the easier it will be for you to create the result you want. When you learn how to show up as a person who over-delivers value, you will receive that value back

10-fold, even if it's not directly received from those you've given your value to.

The added benefits of increased self-confidence and changed beliefs about your value as an employee or an entrepreneur will have a huge ripple effect on your continuing ability to make more money. When you drop the time and effort belief about making money and replace it with the value belief, you open the door to many more possibilities.

As I've mentioned in this chapter, you can always reverse engineer the amount of money you want to make by using the Model. For example, if you currently make $50,000 but you want to make $100,000, you would use the Model in the following reverse order, starting with the result and working your way to the thought:

Result: I make $100,000

Actions: What actions would you need to take? What would you need to start doing? What would you need to stop doing? What value could you provide? What do you need to do to improve your value?

Feeling: How would you need to feel in order to take those actions?

Thought: What believable thought would you need to think in order to feel that feeling?

The bottom line is that the more awareness you have and the greater responsibility you take for your money results, the easier it will be to improve them if you want to. When you work on becoming a Smarter Accountant, you'll be amazed at the results you'll be able to achieve.

If you're still skeptical, let me share this—my mentor, Brooke Castillo of The Life Coach School, has built a $50 million a year business using the Model. Her next big goal is to make $100 million and she's using the Model to do it.

Someone once said to her, "If you can put any result in the Model, why not put $100 million." So she did. She's giving herself 10 years to create that result line and she's doing it one thought, one feeling at a time, allowing her intentional feelings to fuel her actions.

She may not be an accountant, but she's a smart businesswoman who knows the power of a managed brain.

CHAPTER NINE: IF I'M SO SMART, WHY ARE MY RELATIONSHIPS SO DIFFICULT?

Rob's Story

Rob was a CPA and a partner in a small accounting firm. He loved the work that he did but was having a difficult time with various relationships in his life, particularly with some of his clients, his business partner, his wife, and one of his brothers.

It seemed like no matter where Rob turned, there was a struggle with a relationship. Some of his clients were frustrated with him because he didn't return their emails fast enough; he was annoyed at his business partner because of billable hours; his wife didn't seem to appreciate all his hard work; and Rob was missing the closeness he used to have with one of his brothers.

He tried his best to figure out what everyone wanted from him but he became exhausted and resentful. He didn't like how he felt about a lot of the people in his life but didn't know what to do about it.

He also began to feel bad about the contentious relationship he had had with his dad growing up. His dad was a decent provider but was never really there for him in the way that Rob tried to be with his children.

Although his dad passed away years ago, he couldn't help but wonder if things could have been different between them. He wished his dad had been different and that they could have been closer.

Rob figured that this might be one of the reasons he was missing the closeness he used to have with one of his brothers. Growing up, they were inseparable, but over the years they seemed to have drifted apart more and more.

The relationship he worried about the most was with his wife. He had been divorced many years ago and didn't want to make the same mistakes he had made in his first marriage, wanting the love and connection he had always wanted with a romantic partner.

As Rob sat at his desk one Monday morning, he said to himself, "If I'm so smart, why are my relationships so difficult?"

The Truth About Relationships

It doesn't matter whether you're an accounting employee or an entrepreneur, whether you're an introvert or an extrovert, or whether you live alone or are part of a large family, relationships are just a part of life. Relationships form the connections we have with others, whether you realize it or not, are incredibly important for our overall well-being and happiness.

The thing about relationships is that they cannot only give us pleasure—they also influence our long-term health by either causing our brains to release feel-good hormones like dopamine or stress-producing hormones like cortisol. So, for accountants, if you want to have fewer health problems and get more work done, as well as experience less stress, addressing your relationships can be a great place to start.

Interestingly, as humans, we are hardwired to form relationships with others for our survival and the continuation of the species. As humans have evolved from primitive cave dwellers, we have needed to create connections with others in order to have a better chance of surviving by learning, teaching, and supporting each other for the greater good.

In our modern times, relationships are still important for our survival—whether it's a personal relationship with a partner, child, or friend, or a professional relationship with a colleague or client, you most likely have a lot of different relationships with various people in your life. I'm also going to bet that not all your relationships are exactly the way you want them to be.

Maybe you wish your relationship with your partner or spouse was less stressful and more connected, supporting, and loving. Or perhaps you would like your relationship with a particular client or colleague to be less demanding and more easygoing and collaborative.

The truth is that ignoring relationship issues doesn't make them go away. For example, just because you pretend to like your mother-in-law when you're in her company doesn't mean that your true feelings for her don't affect you in various ways, not only personally, but also professionally.

You might be thinking, "Why would my not-so-great relationship with my mother-in-law affect me professionally?" Honestly, you would be surprised by how much your relationships affect you professionally and vice versa.

Thankfully, no matter who the relationship is with or what you believe the problem is, learning a better way to handle any relationship is an incredibly important skill you can learn and apply. I can tell you from experience that, when your relationships improve, life just gets simpler, there's less drama, and it can be happier and much more productive.

The funny thing is that, as accountants, we're so used to focusing on better time management from the perspective of our calendars, but you might be interested to know that your relationships are affecting your ability to get more done in less time, more than you might realize. Your relationships are having an impact on your work as an accountant in so many interesting ways, which is why you must understand the connection.

The most important thing I want you to understand when it comes to relationships is that these are created in our brains by the thoughts we have about other people. The truth is that what creates a relationship at your end is the thoughts you have about the other person, and vice versa.

The reason this is *so* important to understand is that, whenever there are problems in a relationship, the place to begin is with your thoughts. As you already learned in Part One, whenever we're looking at what's created in our lives, including our relationships with others, we always have to go to what we are thinking first and foremost.

As we know from the explanation of the Model, your thoughts create your feelings, those feelings fuel the actions you take or don't take, and those actions are what produce the results that you have in your life. Therefore, every relationship in your life is good, bad, or neutral, based on the thoughts your brain thinks.

While most of us want to blame, or credit, other people for the way we feel, it's *our* job to take responsibility for the thoughts and feelings we're having. The only reason we're experiencing the relationships in our lives in the way we're experiencing them is because of the bubble above our head (i.e. our thoughts), not because of anything people do, don't do, say, or don't say.

Therefore, the secret to improving any relationship is understanding that every relationship you have with a person, place, or thing is based on your thoughts about that person, place, or thing. No matter what state your relationships are in, no one and nothing is ever creating your relationships – that's 100% all you.

This is the best news because it means that you don't need to change or control anyone to improve any relationship. You don't even need the person to be alive to improve your relationship with someone because your relationships were never created by someone else's participation – they were only created by your brain.

So, while it's completely normal to want others to change or to try to control their behavior so that you can feel better, that puts all the focus and responsibility on them. That just leads to outsourcing your feelings to another person, believing that, if they were different, you could feel different.

Whether the relationship is great or not, whether it needs improving or not, every relationship you have is created by your brain and thankfully can be improved by your brain. When you become a Smarter Accountant, you can improve or rescue any relationship.

Unchecking the Box

It doesn't matter whether your relationship is with a person, a pet, or even a company. Again, every relationship you have is based on the thoughts you have. The reason I keep repeating this, and why it's the key to improving any relationship, is because it means that you can do the work without anyone needing to do anything differently.

I understand that this can be confusing because we're so used to believing that other people's actions or inactions are what's contributing to the state of our relationship with them, but that's not the case. Unfortunately, we set ourselves up for disappointment when we put other people in control of our feelings, believing that we would feel better if they changed or did what we wanted them to do.

The issue is that it's so unnecessary and disempowering to go about your life in this way. People have free will to do what they do and the quicker we accept that that's perfectly okay, the better our relationships will be.

Here's the interesting thing—if you think about it when you believe that you would feel a certain way because of another person, then it's understandable that you would want to control or judge their behavior. If you believe your feelings are caused by them, it's no wonder you probably want them to change.

But the issue is that, when we have thoughts about other people, and what they should or shouldn't do to improve our relationship with them, we typically wind up mirroring their behavior. When that happens, we end up producing what we're upset at them about.

Honestly, you could give yourself back so much power to improve any relationship if you just assumed that other people are *not* going to be different from how they are, so now what? Whatever you were wanting to feel if they *did* change is available to you now, based on how you intentionally choose to think.

As a Smarter Accountant, you can dramatically improve any relationship because you understand the power you have. The best part about being a Smarter Accountant is that relationships no longer need to be difficult when you have a managed brain.

Here's what a typical Model looks like for an unmanaged accountant:

Circumstance: Client emailed and said, "I have additional information for my tax return"

Thought: They never get me their information on time

Feeling: Frustrated

Actions: Complain about the client; remember all the times they've done this in the past; start worrying about how to get everything done by the deadline; don't create time boundaries; don't speak to the client about time boundaries; don't look for ways to delegate; waste time arguing with reality; don't look at other options; don't create a plan; put off doing other client work; spin in frustration

Result: I am more likely to not get things done on time

The key here is that the client's email wasn't the problem—it was the thought, "They never get me their information on time" that created the feeling of frustration. The feeling of frustration is never going to drive the actions necessary to have a better relationship with the client and to get things done on time.

Here's what a Model looks like for a Smarter Accountant:

Circumstance: Client emailed and said, "I have additional information for my tax return"

Thought: Their return is simply going on extension

Feeling: Calm

Actions: Accept that they typically have additional information for their return; focus on the plan that was already decided in advance for the clients who previously sent their information on time; email the client to reiterate the firm policy about the deadline for receiving information or their return will automatically go on extension; don't complain about the client; don't take it personally if they are frustrated; allow them to think and feel however they choose to; update the workstream status of the return indicating that additional information was received after the deadline policy; get to work on returns that have all the information in house

Result: I make things simple for me

The Smarter Accountant may have initially felt a sense of frustration with the client, especially if they've done the same thing in the past, but they also know that a feeling of frustration will never give them the result they want. By understanding that circumstances don't cause feelings, they're able to choose how they want to think and feel about the client, making the Smarter Accountant's relationship with the client 100% within their control.

When my coaching clients do the work in the Smarter Accountant Program, they not only improve their relationships with others but, more importantly, with themselves. Just as your relationship with others is based on your thoughts about them, the same thing goes for your thoughts about yourself.

If you want to get to the cause of your difficult relationships, you don't have to look any further than your brain.

Summary

As I mentioned before, your relationships affect more of your personal and professional life than you might realize. I can tell you from my experience, and the experience of my coaching clients, that putting the effort into understanding how to improve your relationships will improve so many aspects of your life.

When I work with clients on the topic of relationships, the tool I teach them is "the Manual". Let me briefly explain this concept. Just as we have instruction manuals for various things we own, we also have instruction manuals that we've unintentionally created for the people in our lives as well.

We have these unwritten manuals in our brains describing what people should and shouldn't do because we believe that, if they followed our manual, then we could feel a certain way. Honestly, there's no shame in having manuals for people because we all have them.

Here are some examples and reasons why we have manuals for others:

- Spouse—your instruction manual for your spouse might state that they remember significant dates in your relationship. The reason you have this in your instruction manual is that you believe that, if they did remember a significant date, you would think "He loves me" and you would feel love. But, on the flip side, if he doesn't remember a significant date, you might think "He doesn't care about our relationship" and feel unloved.

- Boss—your instruction manual for your boss might state that they praise you when you go above and beyond at work. The reason you have this in your instruction manual is that you believe that, if they praise you, then you would think "She really appreciates me" and you would feel appreciated. But, on the flip side, if she doesn't praise you, you might think "Maybe I'm not doing as good of a job as I thought" and feel unappreciated.

- Children—your instruction manual for your children might include them always making their bed every day. The reason you have this in your instruction manual is that you believe that, if they made their beds every day, you would think "I'm doing a good job raising them" and feel proud. But, on the flip side, if they don't make their beds every day, you might think, "I'm not doing a good job" and feel discouraged.

In each example, you have a thought about them, their actions or inactions, and you feel certain emotions. But, when you base your feelings on whether people follow your manual or not, you are at the mercy of everyone else and are likely to become quite controlling.

The truth is that the only reason you want someone to follow your manual is so that you can feel a certain way. But thankfully, the great news is that you can throw away your instruction manuals because the only thing that needs to change is your thinking—and you are 100% in control of that!

You don't need anyone to do or not do something to feel a certain way because your feelings were only ever created by your thoughts, not by what other people do or don't do. That is the best news I can give you.

When you take responsibility for meeting your own emotional needs, you can let go of the need to change what others think, say, and do. It doesn't mean you can't or don't make requests of others but, when you throw away your manual, your feelings aren't hurt when they don't honor your request.

I promise you that there is incredible freedom in throwing away your manual for others and becoming a Smarter Accountant.

CHAPTER TEN: IF I'M SO SMART, WHY IS WORK AFFECTING MY HEALTH?

Heather's Story

Heather was a hardworking accountant and mom. She wasn't a CPA yet but was planning on doing whatever it took to become a CPA and go as far as she could in her career.

She had always been a good student, took her education seriously, and continually set big goals for herself. She didn't want to just be a great mom, she wanted to be a great accountant, wife, daughter, sister, friend, and member of her community.

From the outside looking in, Heather seemed to have it all together. She did her best to balance her work obligations with her family, her boss valued her, and her family loved her. Heather seemed to be the poster child for "work/life balance", as both a working mom and accountant.

The problem was that Heather was having health issues and wasn't telling anyone about them. She had frequent heart palpitations, she was having difficulty sleeping, her bad eating habits were catching up with her, and she hadn't been following up with her suggested check-ups.

The only reason she saw her family doctor every six months was to have a blood pressure medication renewed. Even though he wanted her to address her various symptoms, she would always reply, "I'm an accountant. I just don't have the time. I'll get to it after this deadline."

The issue was that there was never a time when there wasn't a deadline of some kind. Whenever her anxiety became too much, she would pop a Xanax her doctor had prescribed for her for "emergencies" and, when she realized she wasn't able to focus at work because she hadn't slept well that week, she would pick up some Red Bull to have in the office.

When she was home and feeling stressed, she would binge-watch Netflix, drink an extra glass of wine to help her sleep better, or scroll Facebook to see what everyone else was up to. Heather was used to putting "Band Aids" on her health issues, hoping that they were just temporary.

One day she wound up in the emergency room with what felt like symptoms of a heart attack. She was told by the doctor on call that, although she hadn't had a heart attack, cardiac issues were becoming more dangerous for women who weren't managing their work stress.

As Heather's husband brought her home from the hospital that day, she couldn't help but ask herself, "If I'm so smart, why is work affecting my health?"

The Truth About Your Health

In 2013, the Chartered Accountants Benevolent Association (CABA) reported survey results showing that around 30% of participants admitted to a drinking problem. The key is the word "admitted"; if 30% admitted to having an issue, imagine how many were unwilling to.

Unfortunately, this isn't just an issue for accountants. In a 2016 study of lawyers, nearly three out of four participants reported problematic use of alcohol and drugs to cope with stress, starting as early as at law school.

It doesn't matter whether you are an accountant, a lawyer, or in any other field of work because stress, long working hours, an imbalance between work life and family life can be a breeding ground for overusing things to cope. It could come in the form of sitting with a pint of ice cream once everyone's gone to bed or needing that second glass of wine after dinner; the inability to handle stress has become a bigger issue than ever.

The truth is that mental health has become such an important health crisis that every year during the first week of October the National Alliance on Mental Health participates in raising awareness of mental health issues all across the country. They work to educate the public, fight mental health stigmas, and support those with mental health issues.

While the conversation about mental health is becoming less and less taboo, it's still an issue for many people. The subject of workplace health and well-being is being addressed more because it's becoming an even bigger issue in the accounting and finance professions.

In one study, 30.4% of accountants admitted to suffering from mental health issues and 51% admitted that depression and anxiety leave them dreading going to work. When you add the anxiety accountants feel in their professional life to the guilt, anxiety, and exhaustion most feel in their personal life as well, you have a recipe for potential disaster.

Since there can be a lot of confusion and shame when dealing with anxiety, it's important to understand why you feel this way. There is nothing wrong with you if you feel anxious or overwhelmed—you just haven't been aware of how your problem-solving brain has been creating your life.

One of the big issues when it comes to how work affects your health is that you may have become so accustomed to feeling anxiety and overwhelm that it can become just a normal part of life. Unfortunately, you may have normalized the symptoms or, worse, ignored them altogether.

Depending on how long you've been working in the accounting profession, you may have also experienced the normalization of anxiety from most of the people you work with. Attending an in-person continuing education seminar with other overwhelmed, anxious accountants can seem like a "we're all in this together" club.

The good news is that anxiety is a natural response that your primitive brain has when it senses fear, and it uses this response for your survival. There is nothing wrong with you when you feel anxious because your brain is only trying to protect you from perceived danger.

The bad news is that your brain interprets danger in many more non-dangerous situations than you realize. A tax deadline, a client email, or a change in the tax code can create the same feeling of danger that a saber tooth tiger did when humans lived in caves.

The real problem for accountants is that, from the time you went to school to study accounting, you have been trained to think in very specific ways, and these ways can often create unnecessary stress and anxiety. Your "accountant's brain" has been trained for the problem-solving work you do and, when it goes unchecked, it can become your default way of thinking about everything.

If you've ever been told that you are thinking, talking, or arguing like an accountant, that's what I'm talking about. You have been trained to think in ways that non-accountants don't think and don't understand.

The issue is that being surrounded by other people's problems trains your accountant's brain to see more problems. Because your brain is already a problem-solving machine, when you add that capability to the accounting profession's pressures and expectations, it's no wonder that over 50% of accountants feel anxiety and overwhelm.

No matter how work has affected your health, it can be improved by learning how to manage your brain better. When you become a Smarter Accountant, you can have the awareness of how work is affecting your health and be able to do something about it before it becomes an even bigger problem.

Unchecking the Box

If you checked the box in the Introduction to Part I—your work is affecting your health—I'm going to bet that this is probably something you've been dealing with for a while. But I'm not here to scold you: I'm here to help you.

Interestingly, one of the methods many accountants use to self-medicate when it comes to issues like anxiety is ironically overworking. This creates an unhealthy relationship with work whereby you believe that being anxious is fueling you to get more work done or that it shows that you care about what you are doing.

Unfortunately, like the relationship between an addict and a drug dealer, accounting environments notoriously encourage overworking. The external pressures to do more, learn more, and be more can slowly begin to ignite burnout.

When you add the need to fit into the "accountant mold" in how you think, act, and even dress, to the pressures and expectations in your personal life, all of a sudden that glass or two of wine at the end of the day is appealing. This is also when imposter syndrome can sneak in, whereby you start feeling as though everyone else knows what they're doing except you.

Because you are well trained to always be looking for what seems out of place or inconsistent, you may begin catastrophizing the simplest things. For example, a client sends a simple request for their past three years' tax returns and your brain interprets that to mean that the client is unhappy with your services, they're firing you, and that your boss is going to blame you.

Over time, you may begin to believe that catastrophizing makes you careful, but it can have the opposite effect. Catastrophizing creates stress and anxiety, which then cause distraction, oversight, and mistakes.

As a Smarter Accountant, you can get clear about how work is affecting your health and, more importantly, do something about it. The best part about being a Smarter Accountant is that your health has the chance to improve when you have a managed brain.

Here's what a typical Model looks like for an unmanaged accountant:

Circumstance: Email inbox has 50 new unread messages

Thought: There's no way I can get all this done

Feeling: Anxious

Actions: Complain about all the unread email messages; spin in confusion about what to do first; procrastinate dealing with the email messages; start worrying about how to get all my work done; distract myself by doing other things that aren't related to emails; don't create a plan; don't look for ways to prioritize; waste time; feel more anxious about wasted time; grab medicine for my growing headache; snap at my husband when he calls to ask who's picking up our son; feel pressure in my neck and shoulders

Result: I make it less likely that I can get it all done

The key here is that the email inbox with 50 new unread messages wasn't the problem—it was the thought, "There's no way I can get this all done", that created the feeling of anxiety. If there's anything that will slow down an accountant's productivity and increase their susceptibility to health issues, it's the feeling of anxiety.

Here's what a Model looks like for a Smarter Accountant:

Circumstance: Email inbox has 50 new unread messages

Thought: I just need to focus on one message at a time

Feeling: Patient

Actions: Decide and prioritize which emails are important; forward and delegate emails that I don't need to deal with; set aside 1 hour of Focus Time to answer emails that require a brief response; calendar remaining emails; swipe remaining emails into "Next" folder to create a zero inbox; don't waste time worrying how it will get done; don't put added pressure on myself; remind myself that I just need to focus on one message at a time; share my approach with my team so they can benefit from learning how to manage their minds

Result: I focus and get things done one at a time

Because we are a profession that requires communication with other professionals and clients, it's typical to feel anxious when you open your email and there are 50 messages waiting for you, but the Smarter Accountant knows that anxiety is never a useful emotion when it comes to getting things done. By understanding that you can always choose a more helpful feeling, you can reduce your level of stress, anxiety, and overwhelm, improving your health in the process.

Smarter Accountants don't have fewer problems in their career but, instead, have a much better way of dealing with those problems.

When you become a Smarter Accountant, you understand that, by unchecking a lot of the boxes in the Introduction to Part One, you make it possible to have a much healthier, happier, and balanced life.

Summary

No discussion dealing with health issues for accountants can avoid the elephant in the room—burnout. As a profession, we are in big trouble when it comes to burnout, especially in the post-pandemic world that we live in.

Because accountants tend to normalize their struggles, here are some of the signs of burnout that you might want to be aware of:

- Beginning to feel a lack of energy.
- Trouble falling asleep or staying asleep.
- Lack of focus or forgetfulness.
- Prone to catching whatever cold is going around the office.
- Feeling on edge.
- Feeling hopelessness.
- More tense and irritable than usual.
- Loss of enjoyment.
- Noticing a good deal of negative self-talk.
- Isolating yourself.
- Not able to be as productive as usual.

For all the highly intelligent, often high-achieving, perfectionistic accountants reading this book, the road to burnout can happen at any time in your career, whether you are in public or private accounting. For those of you who are afraid to acknowledge that you're getting burned-out, it's okay: it doesn't need to be a dirty little secret any longer.

There is no shame in the fact that you are experiencing burnout, but I also want you to know that it doesn't have to be as normal as you may have been led to believe. There is a way to reduce burnout so that you can live the happy, balanced life that you desire and deserve, without having to give up on the career you've worked so hard for.

Thankfully, the coaching clients who go through the Smarter Accountant Program learn hands-on that, when they believe something or someone is going to be the solution to their feelings of burnout, they're setting themselves up to fail because it isn't anything outside of them that's creating the feeling of burnout. Therefore, by getting a better handle on what causes burnout, they can avoid it.

The truth is that, because your body is only doing what it's supposed to do, which means that it's responding to your brain—all those beliefs about how accountants are supposed to be busy, and all those conversations and justifications for why you feel burned-out, are wrapping you up in a tight web of what I like to call "burnout advocacy". Whenever you or others legitimize burnout, you strengthen the neural pathways in your brain, causing your brain to look for more reasons why you should feel burned-out.

I promise you that, although burnout appears to be normal, it's unnecessary.

In order to reduce burnout, you first need to pay attention to how you think about the people, places, and things in your life, and question what you are indulging in, in your mind. What is the story that is on a rinse and repeat cycle in your brain?

The second thing that will help you reduce burnout is to stop avoiding and procrastinating in making decisions, whether they're big or small. Nothing is more draining to you both mentally and physically than a lack of decision-making skills.

The third thing that will help you reduce burnout is an expression I heard on a podcast – "overworking in an unproductive effort". What it means to overwork in an unproductive effort is knowing you have things you need to get done but then allowing yourself to get distracted by other things.

And the last way that will help you reduce burnout is to have better boundaries. When you're overly available, overly accommodating, or trying to please everyone, you are the one who suffers in the end with burnout.

So, no matter how work is affecting your health, just know that, by becoming a Smarter Accountant, you have much more control in managing your brain.

CHAPTER ELEVEN: IF I'M SO SMART, WHY DO I STRUGGLE WITH SELF-CONFIDENCE, SELF-DOUBT, AND IMPOSTER SYNDROME?

Adam's Story

Adam had been a CPA for over 10 years and had recently realized that he felt stuck at his job. He had graduated Magna Cum Laude and got a job right out of college with one of the Big 4 public firms but wasn't sure whether he wanted to stay in public accounting or switch to private.

While he was getting a lot of experience and training, he was torn about whether he was ready to leave, even though he wasn't happy. He didn't mind the hard work and accepted the work-life imbalance that others were frustrated with.

What Adam was struggling with was a lack of self-confidence, even though he had done well up until now. He was secretly afraid of doing anything outside his comfort zone.

On a daily basis, he felt some degree of self-doubt, both in his professional and personal life. His girlfriend was hinting at getting married and Adam just couldn't commit because he wasn't sure he could be the husband, provider, or eventual father to their children that she hoped he would be.

Sometimes, when he was at work, he had this feeling that someone was going to figure out that he didn't know what he was doing. He had heard this referred to as "imposter syndrome" and that's exactly what it felt like—that he was a fraud and an imposter, just waiting for someone to uncover his secret.

The most recent incident was when a client emailed asking a question about their quarterly financial statement and the comparative gross profit percentage. The client was questioning the validity of the analysis and Adam just froze—he didn't know what to do or what to say.

He not only doubted his abilities but also beat himself up for not being able to answer the client right away, and he was sure that he would get fired. He was so rattled by the client's questions that he felt like calling in sick the next day, just to avoid having to deal with his self-doubt.

As Adam thought about how to handle the situation, he said to himself, "If I'm so smart, why do I struggle with self-confidence, self-doubt, and imposter syndrome?

The Truth About Self-Confidence, Self-Doubt, and Imposter Syndrome

Since on the surface, it would appear that self-confidence wouldn't be an issue for you, then what's the problem? From the outside looking in, you've got what it takes to have a successful career as well as a successful life. So what's the issue?

Interestingly, all of these assumptions are exactly the reason why self-confidence can be an issue for accountants. The reason is that your intelligence, outward achievements, accolades, and successes aren't responsible for your self-confidence, or lack of.

The key to self-confidence isn't found in the number of professional designations after your last name, the school you attended, your IQ, or your technical acumen—it's found in learning how to manage and master your brain. If you haven't learned how to manage your brain, then it's no wonder you may have issues with self-confidence, self-doubt, and imposter syndrome.

What often happens for accountants is that you believe that your accomplishments will finally give you self-confidence, so you try things like working longer and harder, taking more continuing education classes, or trying to please everyone. The issue is that, when you try to fix self-confidence by creating something external, it doesn't last.

Unfortunately, if you think that something like getting a promotion will build your self-confidence, you will most likely wind up still feeling insecure in the new position, often faced with more imposter syndrome. The reason this happens is that your outer circumstances don't create the feeling of self-confidence.

Getting a promotion, finding a mate, or receiving a positive yearly review are the effects, and not the cause, of your self-confidence. The truth is that, If you didn't have self-confidence before going after these achievements, you'd quickly fall back into your old belief system because beliefs don't change without some work.

That's why achieving the professional status of CPA, or any other professional designation, won't build self-confidence if you haven't changed your underlying beliefs about yourself. If you struggle with self-confidence, it's because you haven't addressed the cause.

When it comes to imposter syndrome, if you've ever felt like you don't belong or that friends or colleagues are going to discover that you don't deserve your job or your accomplishments, you are not alone. An estimated 70% of people experience the feelings of being an imposter at some point in their lives.

Still not sure whether you suffer from imposter syndrome? See if any of these apply to you:

- Do you have great difficulty delegating?

- Do you feel like your work must be 100% perfect, most of the time?

- Do you feel like you haven't truly earned your title, despite numerous degrees and achievements?

- Were you told frequently as a child that you were the "smart one" in your family or peer group?

- Do you often avoid challenges because it's so uncomfortable to try something you're not great at?

- Do you feel you need to accomplish things on your own?

- Do you feel like you still don't know "enough" even if you've been in your role for some time?

Whether it's your role as an accountant or in any other area of your life, imposter syndrome creates the feeling that everyone around you is smarter, works harder, or does a better job than you do. You may know rationally that you are good at what you do and that you are a good person, but you can't help feeling fear that someone's going to discover some hidden truth.

Thankfully, becoming a Smarter Accountant can help with all that. When you understand the source of your lack of self-confidence, self-doubt, and imposter syndrome, you'll begin to see yourself in a much better light.

Unchecking the Box

As I said before, if you have issues with self-confidence, self-doubt, and imposter syndrome, you're not alone. The funny thing is that most of us tend to think we're the only ones suffering because there's an added layer of shame that we add to an already challenging situation, making us feel even worse.

The truth is that imposter syndrome often comes from social conditioning. Most young girls are taught at an early age to second-guess themselves, to be self-critical, and to earn outside validation. Most young boys are taught to win at all costs and to be strong no matter what, even when they feel weak.

Another place imposter syndrome can start is with the messages you received from your parents. Your well-meaning parents might have seen your aptitude in a certain area that they valued or that they believed society valued, and then strongly encouraged your performance in that area.

For example, if you were taught that your intelligence is what is valued, bringing home a B- on a math test may have elicited your parents saying, "You can do better, I know you can", reinforcing your belief that you're not good enough. This is often the case with high-achieving individuals who are frequently taught that their intelligence is what they should be most proud of.

What eventually happens, after social and parental conditioning, is that you don't believe the positive things others think or say about you. Your negative-biased brain tells negative stories about your achievements and warps the facts to support its negative beliefs.

As I shared in a previous chapter, there's a part of your brain (the Reticular Activating System) that looks for proof of what you believe. This is great if you have self-confidence and don't suffer from imposter syndrome, but it's not so great if you do.

As with each of the boxes that you might have checked in the Introduction in Part One, awareness is always the first step in dealing with any issue. There's no shame in feeling a lack of self-confidence, self-doubt, and suffering from imposter syndrome, but there's also something you can do about it.

The good news is that the Model can improve it all because self-confidence goes in the feeling line of the Model. As I previously explained, everything below the circumstance line in the Model is within your control. Therefore, the feeling of self-confidence is within your control by what you choose to think about yourself.

As a Smarter Accountant, you will understand why you're feeling a lack of self-confidence, self-doubt, and imposter syndrome and, more importantly, be able to do something about it. It's important to understand that, although the lower, Toddler part of your brain is always going to offer you negative-biased thoughts, by becoming a Smarter Accountant you know how to use the higher, Supervising Mother/Father part of your brain more often, improving your self-confidence in the process.

Here's what a typical Model looks like for an unmanaged accountant:

Circumstance: Boss asked me to do a presentation for the team

Thought: I'm going to fail at this

Feeling: Self-doubt

Actions: Immediately want to say no; spin in confusion about what to say; procrastinate coming up with ideas for the presentation; worry about what others will think of me; think about the times I didn't do well in presentations; don't come up with a plan; don't look for ways I can add value to the team; don't get my other work done because I'm obsessing about the presentation; don't believe in myself

Result: I fail ahead of time

The key here is that the boss asking the accountant to do a presentation for the team wasn't the problem—it was the thought, "I'm going to fail at this", that created the feeling of self-doubt. It's also important to point out that the result of failing ahead of time happens when you're so afraid of failing that your actions, inactions, and reactions lead to an unwanted result—further proof of the thought, "I'm going to fail at this."

Here's what a Model looks like for a Smarter Accountant:

Circumstance: Boss asked me to do a presentation for the team

Thought: I trust that I can figure this out

Feeling: Self-confidence

Actions: I thank the boss for the opportunity; come up with three ideas for the presentation; present the boss with the three options and ask for their input; review what I already know about the chosen topic; research anything that I don't know; calendar the things I need to do for the presentation while also getting my other work done; decide to do a PowerPoint presentation to make it easier on me to present the material; don't worry about what others will think of me; think about what a great opportunity this is for my professional and personal development; look for other opportunities to add value to the team

Result: I figure it all out

The Smarter Accountant understands that self-doubt is always an option, but it isn't going to lead to the results they truly want. With the awareness of how much control they have over what they think and feel, a Smarter Accountant intentionally chooses believable thoughts that produce a more useful feeling.

It's important to understand that you don't need to know how to do something—you only need to trust in yourself and your ability to figure it out. A Smarter Accountant accepts that change and growth are possible because they know that they can rewire their brain to create self-confidence on purpose.

Summary

If you're an accountant who checked the box, indicating that you struggle with self-confidence, self-doubt, and imposter syndrome, you're not alone. Research has found that accountants and finance professionals are prone to imposter syndrome due to the data-driven, analytical work we do, as well as our tendency to be perfectionists.

If you think about it, we're paid to have the answer to other people's problems. The issue though is that the accounting profession has also become a breeding ground for insecure, perfectionistic overachievers.

As I previously mentioned, one of the tools I teach my coaching clients in the Smarter Accountant Program is the term "cognitive dissonance". This describes the common situation whereby you have two conflicting thoughts or beliefs—the old, unhelpful belief that your lower brain automatically thinks, and the new, helpful belief you'd like to think instead.

A simple example would be having a current belief that you hate your body but wanting to get to the belief that you love your body. As you can imagine, if you have practiced the thought over and over again that you hate your body, it's too big a leap to think that you love your body.

Cognitive dissonance is the space between "I hate my body" and "I love my body". It's the discomfort you feel when you're battling between what you currently believe and what you want to believe.

Thankfully, one of the benefits of learning how to become a Smarter Accountant is being aware of cognitive dissonance and being able to manage your brain to the point where your wanted belief becomes possible. By understanding all the ways your unique brain tries to trick you into continuing to believe the old, unhelpful belief, you can gradually lessen its grip and make the new and improved belief realizable.

CHAPTER TWELVE: IF I'M SO SMART, WHY DO I HAVE DIFFICULTY SETTING BOUNDARIES AND DETACHING FROM WORK?

Gina's Story

Gina was a third-generation accountant—her grandfather had been a chief financial officer for a publishing company and her father was the controller for an investment firm. Gina grew up hearing all about hard work, paying your dues, and what it takes to succeed in the accounting profession.

She had attended her family's alma mater, graduated with honors, got a good-paying job right after college, and was now the tax manager at a local mid-sized firm. Although she could have gone down the private accounting route like her grandfather and father had done, Gina wanted to forge a different path for herself while still adhering to her family's work ethic.

She was well respected at her firm and was often asked to be a mentor to the younger female interns and entry-level accountants. They appreciated her guidance and her willingness to help whenever she could.

The issue Gina was dealing with was setting boundaries, especially when it came to her time. Just as her grandfather and father had done, she worked very late hours, initially setting the precedent that she was available 24/7 for her colleagues and her clients.

She was now married, planned on starting a family, and could see the writing on the wall—if she didn't change things now, she would pay the price later. Unfortunately, she was afraid of how others would react once she set a boundary and how that would affect her career.

She had read about setting "healthy" boundaries but had been embarrassed and unsure of what constituted a health boundary. She noticed that, as women's issues were thankfully coming to the forefront of many social injustice movements, more and more women were empowered to stand up for themselves, but she was still left with a lot of questions around the subject of boundaries and detaching from work when she was at home.

What boundary did she want to set? Did she like her reason? How would she handle people's reactions? Would it affect her career? Could she detach from work?

Gina lay in bed one night and thought, "If I'm so smart, why do I have difficulty setting boundaries and detaching from work?"

The Truth About Setting Boundaries and Detaching From Work

While the struggle with work/life balance is not unique to the accounting profession, it is a big problem that isn't getting better. Obviously, there are many factors that have led to the "great resignation" for accountants, but it's also important to understand how a lack of boundaries and the ability to detach from work have contributed to the issue.

One of the things I've noticed over the years is what I refer to as "work martyrdom". This can show up in various ways, such as taking work home so that you can get a jump-start on everyone else, not taking all your paid time off because you're afraid it will look bad, or not being able to delegate because you're worried that no one else can do the work as well as you. Work martyrdom is also sneaky because it's often perceived to be normal, necessary, or, even worse, rewarded.

As I shared in Chapter 2—If I'm So Smart, Why Do I Work Too Many Hours?—the issue with work martyrdom is that it hurts you and your career more than you realize. The perceived need to work harder than everyone else creates less productivity.

I want you to hear this—the person who stays the latest, works the most hours, or has no time boundaries, doesn't necessarily get more work done than everyone else. More hours spent working does not equate to more work done or higher-quality work done.

To get even more real with you, you could have the most billable hours and that still doesn't mean you'll be the best or that you will necessarily be considered valuable. What typically accompanies work martyrdom is frustration, resentment, and burnout, none of which will help you achieve the success you want.

The issue is that we can often get swept up in the tidal wave of other accounting overachievers and perfectionists, believing that more and more sacrifice is necessary while gasping for air as the wave takes us under, leading to full-blown burnout. The issue is that what's left when the tidal wave of work martyrdom subsides is often health issues, damaged relationships, overwhelm, unhappiness, and resentment.

When work martyrdom seeps into your life, it can become like a poisonous gas that is undetectable until after it's done its damage. Just like we have carbon monoxide detectors in our homes because humans can't smell deadly carbon monoxide, you should know the signs of work martyrdom and be able to detect it before it's too late.

It's important to understand that, if you also checked the box "I struggle with self-confidence, self-doubt, and imposter syndrome", the chances are that you're also probably being a work martyr to try to overcome that insecurity. Feeling inadequate and insecure then leads you to take on more, believing that working harder will somehow alleviate those feelings of insecurity.

When it comes to setting boundaries, it's important to understand that it's not only about setting boundaries with people—you also need to learn to set boundaries with yourself and with your time. One of the biggest issues that I see for accountants is setting time boundaries.

When you can learn how to set time boundaries and commit to them, you'll be amazed at how much better you feel about your day. When you set time boundaries, you improve your relationship with time, you honor your values, you get clear about your priorities, and you create a balanced life.

By learning how to set and commit to your time boundaries, you make it much easier to have a balanced day, week, or year, and you lessen the fatigue that comes with making too many decisions about how you spend your time. And one of the best benefits is that you also improve your relationship with yourself because, when you honor your commitments to yourself, you strengthen your self-confidence.

If you feel like you can't detach from work, that your time is not your own, or you're constantly wishing there were more hours in the day, time boundaries might be just the thing you need. Not only will you have much better control over your time, you'll also be able to get more done in less time, making it possible to add even more hours to your day.

Thankfully, by becoming a Smarter Accountant, you can learn how to set better boundaries with everything—with people, with yourself, and with your time—as well as learning how to detach from work. The best part is that, when you understand why you do the things you do, you'll also understand how to change that.

Unchecking the Box

If boundaries are an issue for you, you're not alone. Most of us have issues with setting boundaries for good reasons—we've never been taught how and we're worried about what other people will think if we do, or, worse, what the repercussions will be.

The issue is that we can feel uncomfortable setting boundaries because we believe that we then need to control others once a boundary is set. Many of my coaching clients in the Smarter Accountant Program are reluctant to set boundaries because they feel that, in setting a boundary, they then need to try to monitor and change another person's behavior, exhausting themselves in the process.

They feel uncomfortable drawing a line in the sand and are confused, or emotionally drained, by the idea that they then have to police that line and stop others from crossing over it, or they fear other people's reactions to them setting a boundary as well as the idea of having to confront someone. When this happens, it just seems much easier to not set a boundary and then deal with the consequences.

The problem is that this perception of setting a boundary and then needing to control other people's behavior *is* understandably exhausting and futile, but also unnecessary. If you haven't already realized, you cannot control other people—they have their wants, needs, and preferences that are often not in alignment with yours.

The good news is that the way that I teach the subject of setting boundaries is that it's not about what others need to do or not do, it's about what you will do if, or when, a boundary is crossed. It's not about needing to control anyone or anything other than you.

Whatever your issue is with setting boundaries and detaching from work, the Model will be the key because your actions are always within your control based on the feeling that's fueling those actions. The Smarter Accountant uses the Model to become aware of why they're not setting boundaries and detaching from work, and then uses the Model to take the actions necessary for them to have the results they want.

As a Smarter Accountant, you'll be able to set better boundaries, know what to do when a boundary is crossed, and y also be able to manage your brain afterward. Other people can make requests of you and try to cross your boundaries, but you'll know how to create the confidence you need to support yourself and your decisions.

Here's what a typical Model looks like for an unmanaged accountant:

Circumstance: I work in an accounting firm

Thought: If I leave after working 9 daily hours and don't work weekends, I'm not dedicated

Feeling: Worried

Actions: Stay later than I want; work weekends even when it's not required; worry about what other people will think if I set a boundary; don't set a boundary; don't detach from work; get distracted; don't get more done in less time making it possible to leave; don't prove that my value doesn't equal the amount of time I'm working; don't come up with a plan; don't believe it's possible to be dedicated and leave after 9 hours and not work weekends

Result: I'm not dedicated to myself and what I want

The key here is that the action of not setting a boundary came from the feeling of worry, not because you work in an accounting firm. The thought, "If I leave after 9 hours and don't work weekends, I'm not dedicated", is an optional thought, but it's also an unhelpful thought, especially when it comes to setting boundaries and detaching from work.

Here's what a Model looks like for a Smarter Accountant:

Circumstance: I work in an accounting firm

Thought: I give my best at work for 8–9 hours a day during the week

Feeling: Focused

Actions: Do my best when I'm at work; stay focused on my priorities; set time boundaries; do not stay later than I want; do not work weekends; do not worry about what other people will think if I set a boundary; detach from work when I leave; get more done in less time making it possible to leave; continue to prove that my value doesn't equal the amount of time I'm working; always look for a plan to get my work done within 8–9 hours a week; believe it's possible to be dedicated and leave after 9 hours and not work weekends

Result: I make it possible to work 8–9 hours a day during the week

The Smarter Accountant understands that worry is never going to lead to setting boundaries or detaching from work. Ironically, the better you get at setting boundaries, the better you feel and the more you can get done in less time, making it possible to detach from work without experiencing any guilt.

While setting boundaries can be challenging for a lot of people, it's only because you haven't been taught how to do it in a way that has nothing to do with anyone else. A Smarter Accountant understands that a boundary is set for themselves, not for others, and that boundaries are a win-win for everyone.

Summary

I think one of the most uncomfortable things about setting a boundary with someone other than yourself is preparing to have the conversation to verbalize the boundary. While it isn't always necessary or feasible to have a conversation with someone when you're setting a boundary, it's still helpful to know how to handle a possible conversation so that you don't feel so awkward.

The first thing to do before verbalizing your boundary is to understand that a boundary is what *you* will set and presumably abide by, not what the other person needs to do or stop doing. This is such an important distinction because it will allow you to keep the focus on yourself when getting clear about your boundary, but then also when you have a conversation to share what your boundary is.

Basically, a boundary is not about what the other person needs to stop doing—it's about what your preference is and what you'll do if the boundary is crossed. Thankfully, it's not your job to control or change other people's behavior, but the beauty in setting a better boundary is knowing that the boundary is *for* you, not *to* them.

For example, you're not telling your friend she can't be late for your lunch dates anymore when you set a boundary with her. You're just letting her know that her lateness doesn't work for you and what you will do the next time she's late—she doesn't need to change, you just have a plan if it happens again.

You're not telling your boss that he shouldn't send emails to you over the weekend when you set a boundary with him. You're just letting him know that you have chosen the weekends to be email-free time with your family and that you won't be answering emails until Monday morning—he can keep sending emails but you have a plan if it happens again.

The beauty in this is that your friend gets to continue being late as much as she wants without you needing to change her behavior or getting angry with her, and your boss gets to send emails whenever he wants. Other people have the power to do whatever they want, but so do you.

When setting a boundary with yourself, you have to understand why you're setting a boundary and then expect that you'll probably try to cross your boundary as well. For example, just because you set a time boundary that you're going to leave the office by 5 p.m. doesn't mean your lower, Toddler brain won't say, "Just one more minute. I need to finish this."

A Smarter Accountant knows that boundaries need to be set and they're prepared as to what to do if they, or someone else, tries to cross the boundary. It's about having a compelling reason and liking your reason—that's what leads to setting boundaries and detaching from work.

CHAPTER THIRTEEN: IF I'M SO SMART, WHY DON'T I FEEL HAPPIER/BETTER?

Brian's Story

Brian was the owner of a small firm and heading towards retirement, looking to sell his practice to one of his colleagues. Although he had been looking forward to his retirement for years, he was surprised at how unhappy he was.

Looking back over his life and his career, he could see a pattern—when he was younger, he thought that winning the ball game would make him happy; when he graduated from college, he thought that passing the CPA exam would make him happy; when he had children, he thought they would make him happy but he was now seeing that those moments of happiness were fleeting.

When he signed a big client, that meant possibly needing to hire more associates to help with the workload. When he took a day off during the week to play golf with some colleagues, that meant he would probably have to come in on the Sunday to make up the time. When he went on vacation with his family, that meant he had to trust that the office would run smoothly without him.

He was well respected by his peers and had been asked to speak at various CPE conferences because of his expertise in cryptocurrency accounting. He was even considering teaching a class or two at a local college when he retired, not wanting his knowledge to go to waste.

The interesting thing was that Brian had never considered himself a pessimist but he was seeing his life through a "glass-half-empty" lens. His wife had started to point it out to him, making him annoyed at first, but then he realized she was right—he wasn't as happy as he'd like to be or thought he should be.

He had to admit that, at various stages throughout his life, he believed that something or someone would make him happy, feeling disappointed when it didn't happen. He had a level of success he had only dreamed about, had a loving wife, beautiful children, and was financially secure, so what could be the problem?

As he left for work one Monday morning he asked himself, "If I'm so smart, why don't I feel happier?"

The Truth About Feeling Happier/Better

As children, we can't wait to get that special toy we've been waiting for all year. Remember when you felt the thrill of anticipation, excitement, and happiness, believing that getting that desired gift would be the cause of your happiness?

No matter what holiday we celebrate or what age we are, we often wish those great feelings could last throughout the year. The truth is that most of us are taught at a very early age to want something outside ourselves to feel better, associating our feelings with people, places, and things.

The interesting thing though is that, as we grow up, the desire grows even bigger, the programming gets stronger, and we end up feeling worse when we don't get what we think we want. As adults, we understand that being happy all the time is not feasible, but we also can't help wanting things to make us feel better.

No matter how old we are, we're still programmed to believe that losing those last 10 pounds, finding that perfect match, owning that shiny red car, or going on that tropical vacation will be the answer to our happiness. If only we could achieve that level of success, see that balance in our retirement account, or have that extra week's vacation, then we'd feel better.

As an accountant, I think it's fascinating that the number one thing most people believe will make them happier is having more money. But consider this—have you ever wondered why there are so many unhappy, wealthy people?

I can honestly tell you in my 30+ year career in public accounting and being exposed to many high-net-worth clients, money cannot buy you happiness or love. I can also tell you that the happiest person I have ever met in my life was a man who handed out towels at a resort in Jamaica and who lived with his family in a mud hut on the hillside with no running water.

The simple reason we want the things we want is that we believe we will feel better in the having of them. But if you checked the box that said, "You wish you could feel happier/better", I'm going to share something that has made all the difference to me and my coaching clients in the Smarter Accountant Program—your feelings don't come from people, places, or things: your feelings come from your thoughts.

I explained this in Part One and have reintroduced it throughout this book, but it bears repeating—circumstances don't cause feelings. The only thing that ever causes a feeling is your thoughts.

The reason this matters is because you don't need anything to be different for you to feel how you want to feel. But, more importantly, how you currently feel has nothing to do with anyone or anything other than the thoughts you're thinking.

When I point this out to my coaching clients, it can be a bit confusing at first because we're so used to connecting our feelings with things outside of us. For example, we believe we're mad because a person cut us off in traffic or we're glad because we got a promotion at work.

The truth is that there was a thought that preceded a feeling, but most of the time we're completely unaware that that's what is happening. We automatically associate the feeling with the thing and give it blame or credit.

It's no wonder that we want things to be different so that we can feel a certain way. We've become so accustomed to blaming things for how we feel.

Thankfully, if you want to feel happier/better, all you have to do is manage your brain. As a Smarter Accountant, you understand that the key to your happiness lies in your higher brain, not in your bank balance or whatever you believed up until now is responsible for making you feel better.

Unchecking the Box

Before I share how to uncheck the box, I want to point out that, if you suffer from depression, there's no shame in seeking help. There are many resources for accountants, nationally and locally, so please don't ignore an issue that might need clinical intervention.

But, if you experience a low level of unhappiness or don't believe you need help for depression, then let me share some things that might be helpful. Anytime you can learn a new way of understanding how your brain works, it can put many pieces of the puzzle together that you might otherwise have thought were unfixable.

The first step in feeling better is taking responsibility for how you feel right now. Taking responsibility means looking at how you currently feel and telling yourself, "I am creating this", in a non-judgmental, accepting way.

Taking responsibility is just an exercise in curiosity. It's acknowledging how you feel and then asking yourself what thought is creating that feeling.

It's important to understand that blaming circumstances for how you feel is also how you stay stuck. If you want to feel better, you first have to own the fact that how you feel is due to a thought your brain is offering you. What is the thought that's creating your current feeling?

The second step is to simply decide how you want to feel. If you don't want to feel how you're currently feeling, then how do you want to feel? Calm, happy, motivated, hopeful? I typically suggest that my coaching clients envision a giant buffet table with unlimited feelings—which one would you like to pick?

Now that you've chosen a feeling, you just need to choose a thought that will create that feeling. What believable thought can you think that will create your chosen feeling? Is it "Things are always working out for me", "I am blessed", "I can do hard things", or "I can't wait to see what happens"?

If you're like most people, you probably didn't realize that you always get to choose how you feel, even if you choose to feel sad, like when someone dies, or feel mad, like when someone hurts you.

A Smarter Accountant knows that part of being human is feeling all emotions, but they also know that the only thing creating their emotions is their thoughts. They take responsibility for how they're feeling and they live more intentional, happy lives.

Here's what a typical Model looks like for an unmanaged accountant:

Circumstance: My spouse said, "You don't spend enough time at home"

Thought: She's never satisfied with me

Feeling: Frustrated

Actions: Argue with spouse; complain about her; avoid being home by staying late at work; look for proof of all the other ways she's never satisfied; don't see her point of view; don't discuss the issue with her; don't come up with a plan together; stay up late watching TV alone; let work obligations come first; don't prioritize time at home; look for all the things she does that I'm not happy with

Result: I'm not satisfied with her

As you can see, the feeling of frustration wasn't caused by the spouse's comment, it was caused by the thought, "She's never satisfied with me." So often, we blame our feelings on the circumstances in our lives, but then create results that perpetuate the feeling we don't want to have.

Here's what a Model looks like for a Smarter Accountant:

Circumstance: My spouse said, "You don't spend enough time at home"

Thought: I guess she wants to spend more time with me

Feeling: Love

Actions: Acknowledge what she's feeling; discuss a plan that we can both be happy with; look for ways that I can spend more time at home; make plans to spend more one-on-one time with her and each of the kids; figure out a way to make family come first without it affecting work; look for all the ways I love her and the time we spend together

Result: I am more likely to spend more time at home

The Smarter Accountant understands that their optional thoughts are what create their feelings, not the circumstances in their life. They know that their feelings are 100% within their control and choose to be more intentional with their thoughts so they can be more intentional with their feelings.

The key is understanding that how you feel on a daily basis is what creates the actions and the results you have in your life. By getting clear about the feelings you would like to feel, you can change your results in a big way.

Summary

Now that I've shared how to feel happier/better, I want to also point out that having what you would consider negative emotions is completely normal. Your human experience is supposed to be 50/50—50% of the time you'll feel positive emotions and 50% of the time you'll feel less than positive emotions.

I think one of the things that has made a lot of people unhappy is that they feel they have to be in pursuit of happiness. They think that happiness is the goal and that, when they're not achieving it, there must be something wrong with them.

The issue is that when you feel bad for feeling bad, you just add another layer of judgment on top of already feeling bad. For example, you might feel frustrated by the fact that you're feeling overwhelmed, adding a layer of judgment on yourself for feeling overwhelmed.

What if you made it okay to feel bad? What if you accepted that this is the part where you're experiencing the 50% of life that doesn't feel great? What if you allowed it to be okay that you don't feel happy? How would that feel?

If you're anything like my coaching clients, it's probably a big relief to not judge yourself for how you're feeling. There is an incredible sense of freedom in accepting that this is just the way it is right now, without adding blame or shame.

The amazing thing about letting go of the pursuit of happiness is that it's much easier to achieve it then. When you feel okay about not feeling okay, you increase your ability to feel better.

Isn't that interesting? The better you feel about not feeling happy, the easier it is to feel better.

My suggestion is to accept how you feel and then know that the Model is available whenever you're ready to feel better. The Smarter Accountant accepts that their life is going to be 50/50, they don't make themselves wrong for their humanness, and they feel better in the process.

CHAPTER FOURTEEN: IF I'M SO SMART, WHY (FILL IN THE BLANK)?

Your Story

As I said at the beginning of this book, you're already smart or you wouldn't be an accountant. No one is denying your intelligence, but what I have hopefully been able to show you is that you're not being as smart as you could be.

To make it clear what it means to be a Smarter Accountant, I only chose 12 issues that accountants typically deal with but—let me assure you—there is SO much more that I, and the Model, can help you with:

- If I'm so smart, why am I not getting the promotion I want?
- If I'm so smart, why am I so disorganized?
- If I'm so smart, why do I have such a hard time dealing with difficult people?
- If I'm so smart, why do I feel so much guilt?
- If I'm so smart, why can't I achieve that goal?
- If I'm so smart, why can't I solve my problems?

The best part about becoming a Smarter Accountant is that there is nothing you can't manage when you learn how to manage your brain. As your life changes (and it will), learning the skill of being a Smarter Accountant means that there's nothing you can't handle.

If you're anything like most of the accountants I speak to, you don't like change. While it's completely normal to resist change (remember—your Toddler brain likes things to stay the same), it's also like paddling upstream when you don't know how to manage it.

Thankfully, you now know the secret to having the career and the life you want because, when you learn how to manage your brain, you can manage everything else. There's no situation that can't be managed with the Model.

So what's your story going to be? How will others describe you as an accountant and as a person? Will you continue to be a "typical" burned-out accountant, or will you begin to make the shift to becoming a Smarter Accountant?

The world needs Smarter Accountants. I hope you choose to become one.

PART III - THE PLAN

CHAPTER ONE: THE FINAL STORY

Jim's Story

Jim was a partner in an accounting firm and a father to 5 young children - 2 boys and 3 girls. He worked hard to support his wife and children, doing what he could to afford a home in a good school district.

As a partner in a firm at only 38 years old, with a stay-at-home wife, 5 children, and a new home, he was likely very stressed. He probably tried not to bring that stress and overwhelm home, but it couldn't have been easy.

His wife must have been concerned for his health, especially with him having had a heart attack the prior year.

One day Jim and his family went to the beach with some friends, and he had the opportunity to go water skiing on one of his friend's boats. It seemed like something fun to try and a nice way to relax and detach from the pressures of work.

Unfortunately, that day Jim had a heart attack on the beach, in front of his wife and young children, and didn't survive. He left a young wife with 5 young children, trying to make sense of what happened.

As more studies have shown the effects of stress on the body, it's safe to assume stress most likely contributed to his heart attacks at such a young age. Stress was probably poisoning his body and had unfortunately become a silent killer.

The truth is that Jim's story is personal to me because he was my husband's father. I never got to meet him, but I have been married to the 8-year-old boy who watched his father die on the beach that day.

When my husband told me the story of his dad's death, I couldn't help but wonder how many accountants have no idea how much stress is detrimentally affecting them. How many accountants need to be burned out, or worse, before something changes?

Whether you have children or not, please do not let Jim's story become your story. Consider becoming a Smarter Accountant not just for your sake, but for everyone's sake.

CHAPTER TWO: THE LIFE OF A SMARTER ACCOUNTANT

Hopefully, you've gained some insight into how your brain works and what it's like to be a Smarter Accountant. Maybe you resonated with some of the various stories of accountants throughout the book who have struggled with the same issues you have.

I want you to know that I don't just teach and coach; I live this. The reason I wrote this book is to help accountants see that there is a better way - the Smarter Accountant way.

I have wanted to be a thought leader in the accounting profession for quite a while, and this book is the culmination of the wisdom I've gained and applied over the years. Here's what I want you to know - there is a better way, but you have to be willing to be open to it.

For far too long, accountants have bought into some very limiting, damaging beliefs that have continued to be perpetuated throughout the profession. We have so many people questioning whether they want to be an accountant or decide to retire early.

I've seen it repeatedly - accountants are not only on the verge of burnout but also fully immersed in it. I'm here to tell you that it is not only fixable but also unnecessary to be so stressed, overwhelmed, and burned out.

The truth is that things like the work we do, the companies and the clients we serve, the changes to the IRS tax code, and the state of the economy, are not responsible for why we feel the way we do. If you've learned anything from this book, I hope you take away the fact that circumstances don't cause feelings.

This is important because it gives you all your power back - to have the career and the life you truly want. The people, places, and things in your life are all neutral; therefore, your unmanaged brain is causing all the issues you're dealing with.

Any of the boxes you checked in the Introduction to Part I are all caused by your brain. Hopefully, you've learned throughout this book that when you change the cause, you also change the effect.

If you want to uncheck those boxes, you must become aware of how your unique accountant brain is thinking and how those thoughts create how you feel, what you do and don't do, and ultimately create your results. It all comes from an unmanaged brain.

EVERYTHING changed professionally and personally once I learned The Model and began to apply it to my life. Some of the changes include:

- I rarely experience stress, even during tax season
- I work only the hours I want to work
- My life is incredibly balanced
- I get more done than anyone else in less time
- I am highly productive and efficient
- I am much better about not comparing myself to others

- I choose to interpret things as feedback rather than criticism
- I'm making more money than I've ever made
- My relationships have improved dramatically
- My health is better than it's been in years
- I have more self-confidence than I've ever had
- I set healthy boundaries and have no problem keeping them
- I am happier than I've ever been

The best part is that you can do the same. You'll not only be able to uncheck the boxes I outlined in this book, but you can uncheck any box that has become an issue and improve any area of your career and life.

CHAPTER THREE: GAINING A COMPETITIVE ADVANTAGE

While I would love to work with every accountant to help them uncheck the boxes affecting them personally and professionally, I know it's probably going to take some time to get the word out about being a Smarter Accountant. Until that happens, guess what you'll gain by learning what I've taught in this book and possibly working with me? A competitive advantage.

We all know that the accounting profession is for intelligent individuals. But it's also a highly competitive profession where being a small fish in a big pond can often derail one's goals and aspirations.

What if there was a way to be a big fish? What if you could become an accountant that stands out among your peers? What opportunities would be possible?

- If you knew how to eliminate stress and overwhelm so that you could easily handle deadlines, how would you stand out from the crowd of burned-out accountants?

- If you had self-confidence and stopped using the number of hours you work as a sign of your value, what else would make you more valuable?

- If you had incredible time management, how much more could you get done in less time than everyone else?

- If you could be more productive, how would you excel?

- If you stopped comparing yourself to others and believing you fall short, what opportunities would you go after?

- If you could see feedback as information instead of criticism, how could you use that feedback to grow in your career?

- If you focused on ways to continue adding value, how much money do you think would be possible to make, and how much more would someone be willing to pay for your value?

- If you understood how to have good relationships with everyone and the importance of emotional adulthood, how much better would you be at managing people?

- If you knew how to stop having work affect your health, how would you show up differently than everyone else?

- If self-doubt and imposter syndrome were no longer an issue, what goals would you go after?

- If you knew how to set better boundaries, how much more effective would you be at your job?

- If you felt happier, how would you stand out from the crowd?

No matter which boxes you previously checked, there's no denying that becoming a Smarter Accountant will give you a competitive advantage in so many ways. Whether or not that's important to you, I hope I've given you enough ways to see how you can have a successful accounting career on your terms and stand out from the crowd.

Bottom line - you're already smart, but you're underutilizing your brain. Learn that skill, and you'll be unstoppable!

CHAPTER FOUR: WHY THIS MATTERS

Throughout this book, I've shared the story of different accountants who have struggled with the same things you might be struggling with, but why does this all matter? The accounting profession will be fine, with or without Smarter Accountants, so why write an entire book trying to teach something new?

Becoming a Smarter Accountant matters:

- If you want to reduce or eliminate stress dramatically
- If you want a competitive advantage
- If you want to create more time for what matters to you - the things and the people you love
- If you want to achieve any goal you set, whether it's personally or professionally
- If you want a sustainable career and a balanced life
- If you want to ward off burnout
- If you want to create a legacy that you can be proud of
- If you want to make a positive impact on others
- If you want to be an example of what's possible (my personal favorite!)
- If you want to change what's not working
- If you want to make a difference

If you are an older generation accountant, I hope that you are open to challenging your limiting beliefs. You earned it.

If you are at a mid-career point in your accounting career, I hope you begin to create a vision of what you'd like for your life and career moving forward. You deserve it.

If you are just starting your career, or still an accounting student, I hope that you forge your unique path and do things differently than those who have come before you who are experiencing many of those checked boxes. You are the future.

I hope this book helps shine a light on what hasn't worked but also helps keep your focus on what you'd like to see in the future. You can do that by starting to ask powerful questions:

- What do you value?
- What actions do you need to start or stop doing?
- How do you need to feel to take those actions?
- What do you need to think to create that feeling?

A Smarter Accountant understands that asking and answering these questions daily is how to regain control of their career and life. You are so much more powerful than you realize - you just haven't been aware....until now.

The next natural question is - how do I become a Smarter Accountant? The way I see it, you have two options.

CHAPTER FIVE: THE TWO OPTIONS

We've all heard the saying, "Knowledge is power," but that's not correct. As accountants, we have plenty of knowledge but often feel pretty powerless.

The truth is that ACTION is power. Becoming more knowledgeable is one thing but doing something with that knowledge is much more powerful.

Now that I've given you some of the knowledge to become a Smarter Accountant, you have two options:

- You can take what you've learned in this book and do it on your own.

- You can join **The Smarter Accountant Program** and be coached personally by me.

No matter which option you choose, I hope you don't read this book and then do nothing.

Please don't passively absorb this information and then continue to keep those boxes checked. Whether you make a change for yourself, those you work with, or those you live with, promise yourself you'll do what it takes to become a Smarter Accountant.

Suppose you choose the first option, to take what you've learned in this book and do it on your own. In that case, I suggest you make sure you understand what your unique accountant brain is thinking, be curious, and be willing to separate the facts from your story about the facts and get familiar with whether a thought is helpful.

If you choose the second option, joining **The Smarter Accountant Program**, we'll work together on whatever boxes you checked and I will help you keep it unchecked. You'll get all the personalized coaching and support you need as we explore your accountant brain together and get the results you want and deserve *(you can find out more information by simply going to* www.thesmarteraccountant.com*)*.

No matter which option you choose, I sincerely appreciate you reading this book, and I hope you share it with other accountants. As we each become Smarter Accountants, we not only become an example of what's possible for our peers, but we also can help the next generation of accountants.

I wish every college accounting program, national and state society of accountants, accounting firm, and company encourages accountants to read this book and become Smarter Accountants. As the saying goes, "When you know better, you do better" - the truth is that we can all do better.

If you want to make a difference in your personal and professional life, please consider becoming a Smarter Accountant!

Made in the USA
Columbia, SC
27 October 2022